Praise for 9 *Secrets to Bedroom Bliss*

Written in a style that is both witty and inspiring, this book offers ways to bring vitality and variety to you loving. I recommend it highly.

Susan Campbell, Ph.D., Author of **Getting Real** and **Truth in Dating**

The delightful concept of nine sex archetypes along with detailed examples and excellent writing makes **9 Secrets to Bedroom Bliss** *a fun book to read.*

Betty Dodson, Ph.D., Author of **Orgasms for Two**

What do we all do in the bedroom? Jim and Oona give us an "insider's" peek at our sexuality with more insight, depth and sweetness than few have done before.

Stan Dale Ph.D., Author of **Fantasies Can Set You Free** and creator of the **Love, Intimacy and Sexuality workshops**

If you are looking to spice up your sex life, this book will give you that and more. The nine sexual archetypes provide a palette for pleasure and self-discovery.

Elizabeth Davis, Author of **Women's Sexual Passages: Finding Pleasure and Intimacy at Every Stage of Life**

This lively and enthralling book breaks new ground and shows us a way to love more fully and consciously.

Johanina Wikoff, Ph.D., Author of **The Complete Idiot's Guide to the Kama Sutra**

Match the romantic and the concupiscent together in computer science and transcendental sexuality, put them in bed together, and lo, you're in a state of delirious bliss. Don't miss it!

John Money, Ph.D., Author of **Lovemaps**

9 SECRETS TO BEDROOM BLISS

9
SECRETS
TO
BEDROOM
BLISS

*Exploring Sexual Archetypes to
Reveal Your Lover's Passions and Discover
What Turns You On*

JAMES HERRIOT, Ph.D.
AND OONA MOURIER, Ph.D.

FAIR WINDS
PRESS
GLOUCESTER, MASSACHUSETTS

Text © 2003 by James Herriot and Oona Mourier

First published in the USA in 2003 by
Fair Winds Press
33 Commercial Street
Gloucester, MA 01930

Library of Congress Cataloging-in-Publication Data available

ISBN 1-59233-009-6

10 9 8 7 6 5 4 3 2 1

Cover design by Carol Goodman
Book design by Laura Herrmann Design

Printed and bound in Canada

To my wife, Maren,
I write this as a love letter to you.

To my parents and my children,
I am embraced by your generations.

— J.H.

To the source of all, my gratitude for this teaching.

To my daughter Alodie and the next generation,
may you delight in your sexuality.

To Mingo for your enduring love and friendship.

— O.M.

CONTENTS

Introduction: A Year of Sex Therapy in a Book   11

Lover's Agreement   15

Pop Quiz   17

Chapter One   21
The Nine Sexual Archetypes

Chapter Two   37
The Innocent

Chapter Three   65
The Adventurer

Chapter Four   93
The Sensualist

Chapter Five   117
The Seeker

Chapter Six   135
The Revealer

Chapter Seven   159
The Magician

Chapter Eight   185
The Mystic

Chapter Nine   209
The Nurturer

Chapter Ten   227
The Artist

Afterglow   233

Acknowledgements   245

About the Authors   247

INTRODUCTION

A Year of Sex Therapy in a Book

S ex is fun. And sex is very powerful. Sex can change you and your relationships. Sex can tap into the deepest aquifers of your soul. Sex can revitalize you. It can bring a sparkle to your eyes.

Sexual archetypes are the road map of your sexuality. These archetypes chart the different ecstatic faces you wear during your moments of bedroom bliss. They can illuminate your intimate sublime moments. Sexual archetypes describe the full spectrum of how you can truly make love—engaging, heartfelt, exciting, soulful, beautiful love.

Sexual archetypes represent a paradigm shift in how to think about, live out, and fully enjoy your sexuality.

If you sometimes hold back from full-bore erotic intensity, greater understanding can help open up your sexual self. If your passion is unbounded, knowledge can only make sex more free-flowing and steamy.

SEX THERAPY

It's no wonder that many people seek out sex therapists. Everyone can learn more about sex. But as valuable as professional sex therapy is for many people, it's not for everyone. For many of you, your best teacher is your spouse, partner, or lover. There is so much to be inhaled and learned from your partner. We wrote this book so you can teach these sexual archetypes to each other in the inner sanctum of your bedroom—the very best classroom of all!

Oona is a professional sexologist who devotes most of her time to her sex therapy practice, and Jim is a scientist who's been spending hours at the keyboard writing the words on these pages. This book was born out of thousands of hours of joint collaboration, time spent fleshing out the nuances of each of the nine sexual archetypes. In addition, we have been test-driving the material in this book for 15 years and have applied it abundantly to our personal and professional lives.

Sexual Archetypes

The idea of sexual archetypes is probably in all of us deep down—in our collective psyches as well. Very present, yet not at all obvious.

How did we discover sexual archetypes? Fifteen years ago, we each separately encountered a treasure-like "map" of sexuality drawn as a circle of symbols, a mandala, or "wheel," said to come from indigenous American teachings. It was an epiphany. It knocked our socks off. Maybe the rest of our clothes off, too! The light bulb went on. We were finally able to see into the mythic underpinnings of sexuality, as if we suddenly had X-ray vision. Through this lens, the nine sexual archetypes jumped into view. Oona then began mapping out links between sexual archetypes and traditional sexual science. Together, Oona and Jim over the ensuing years put all the puzzle pieces together that make up this book.

Discovering sexual archetypes corroborated and high-lighted our best intuitions—that sexuality is a mystical journey, complete with the challenges and victories of mythic heroes, guiding us to the very transformation of our souls. Oh, and it's lots of fun, too.

Sexual archetypes live in the realm of direct experience. They're real. You have to touch and taste them. You have to be right there "inside" them. They demand that you embody them. We have used a story combined with explanation to convey the power and beauty of each of the archetypes. We strongly encourage you to practice bringing them out in your own intimate bedroom settings. Like Sleeping Beauty, these archetypes are waiting to be awoken—by you.

MICHELLE, MICHAEL, AND "DR. OONA"

The story line in this book is the journey of Michelle and Michael, a couple discovering these nine sexual archetypes in their own love lives. Their sex therapist? None other than "Dr. Oona" herself. Not to confuse you, but in this book, "Dr. Oona" is both a character in our story and the co-author.

Although Michael and Michelle have graciously volunteered to tell us their story and let us peek into their bedroom, they could be any of us. To quote Michelle:

Maybe it's lucky our names are so similar; that way, we can be thought of interchangeably—even with regard to gender. If you're lesbian, then think of us as women. The same goes for gays, bisexuals, transgenders, intersex, and everybody else. And if you're a couple with four kids, living on a farm in North Dakota, we'd like you to think of us as your next-door neighbors. Come on over.

ONWARD

Turn the pages, and begin your year of sex therapy in a book. And more deliciously, enjoy these yummy sexual archetypes, and each other.

Let us tell you a story, a bedtime story.

— Jim and Oona

LOVER'S AGREEMENT

I understand that I am embarking on a journey which will change me—and us. I will be challenged to push the limits of my normal patterns, and to stretch my beliefs. Together with you, I will travel to faraway enchanting lands. I may go beyond what I thought was possible. I will be by your side and hold you tight. Please hold me tight, too.

I also understand that the gold at the end of our rainbow is renewed vitality, hotter sex, deeper intimacy, and more freedom and ecstasy in our lovemaking. We'll also just plain have more fun hanging out together.

So, looking into your eyes, I agree to dive into the ocean of our sexuality, swim with new sea creatures, and rejoice in the beauty that is truly you, my beloved. I agree to stay present through the journey and communicate my experience kindly.

Love,

_____   _____

Pop Quiz

*T*ake this quiz to discover your "home" sexual archetype. Remember there are no right or wrong answers! Please choose the *one* that best describes you:

1. I like sex when it is playful, light, and fun.

2. I like sex when it is explorative and daring.

3. I like sex when it is passionate and hot.

4. I like sex when we go beyond our comfort zones.

5. I like sex when we share intimate secrets.

6. I like sex when I open doors for my partner.

7. I like sex when it is a mystical experience.

8. I like sex when it is comfortable and close.

9. I like sex when all of life flow is present.

All answers get an A for Aphrodisiac, and…maybe, just maybe, the number you chose is your "home" sexual archetype. Match your choice to the list on the following page.

1. *The Innocent*

2. *The Adventurer*

3. *The Sensualist*

4. *The Seeker*

5. *The Revealer*

6. *The Magician*

7. *The Mystic*

8. *The Nurturer*

9. *The Artist*

Oops—you picked more than one? Well that's OK, too! Stay tuned for more on sexual archetypes and your "home" archetype.

JUST CURIOUS: ARE YOU...

Are you playful during sex? Do you like to play games, dress up, flirt? If this is your idea of fun, you're probably familiar with the *Innocent*.

Are you someone who likes to push the boundaries, challenge what society has taught you about sex, see what you can get away with? If this turns you on, chances are you've met the *Adventurer*.

Do you revel in the sheer bodily pleasure of sex? Do you focus your sexual energies on achieving a fantastic orgasm? If you do, you've enjoyed the *Sensualist*.

Do you like to play with dramatic tension in the bedroom? Have you ever had fantasies of playing with power or bondage? If you have, you've encountered the *Seeker*.

Do you and your partner like to talk about sex? Have you ever revealed deep, dark secrets about your sexuality? If you have, you've been visited by the *Revealer*.

Have you ever helped your lover over a difficult sexual hurdle, and rejoiced to see the sparkle return to your partner's eyes? If you have, you know what it's like to be in the role of the *Magician*.

Have you and your mate ever made love with your minds, bodies, and souls...deep in the cosmos...with the entire universe present? If you have, you know the *Mystic*.

Do you prefer low-key cuddling and snuggling with your mate? If you do, your "home" archetype might be the *Nurturer*.

Can you play your lover like a Stradivarius? If you're adept at all these archetypes—a sexual maestro—you're lucky enough to know the *Artist*.

CHAPTER ONE

Honey, there's a sexual archetype in the bedroom!

THE NINE
SEXUAL ARCHETYPES

"Mathematics is the queen of the sciences.
Sex is queen of the arts."

— James Herriot

Michael and I have been together for four years now. It's been great except for our sex life. I love him. But for a long time, there's been something missing.

Then Dr. Oona told us about sexual archetypes. It changed our lives. We learned how to really dive in and totally enjoy each other.

It's amazing. I'm not sure we'd still be together if we hadn't discovered this! It's as if sex has changed from meat and potatoes to a gourmet feast.

— Michelle

A Dinnertime Parable

It's a sultry Saturday evening. You've invited me to join you at your favorite restaurant uptown. We've been seated by the maitre d' at a cozy, intimate table for two by a moonlit window. Starched napkins adorn the old-world crockery. Candlelight flickers in your glistening eyes. The proud waiter arrives to take our orders. What is your desire?

Yes, I should like a small sack of pastry flour, three raw eggs, a stick of butter, and some sugar, if you please.

Excuse me?

We would *never* order raw ingredients at a fine restaurant. No! We would order an entire sumptuous dinner, a song of flavors, a presentation of exquisite beauty. Our conversation would be guided by the tingles of our palates, the swish of delectable smooth wines, the ambience conveyed in the soft folds of the burgundy draperies.

This book is about the *dinner*, not the *ingredients*.

There are lots of excellent books on ingredients—sexual techniques and positions. Ingredients are important. Good chefs use quality ingredients. Michelangelo used the best paints. Sexual ingredients are important, too. They are a great starting point. But now it's time to put the raw pieces together, assemble the many parts into an integrated whole, cook up a full-on sumptuous, sexual feast in your private bedroom hideaway.

So what does all this fine dining have to do with sexual archetypes?

Your Sexual Archetype

Sexual archetypes are about:

- A transformative journey

- Discovering new landscape in your sexuality
- Expanding your sexual language and understanding the whole, not just the parts
- All of you: your emotions, bodies, minds, spirits, and sexuality
- Freedom to be yourself in your unique way, choice, and awakening
- Deeper and more powerful connection with your partner
- Fun, sex, juice, sizzle, excitement, adoration, orgasms!

Sexual archetypes are about the whole enchilada, the whole banquet, the five-course dinner, the fully soulful sexual experience. And just as we are able to select the restaurants, we get to choose the archetype. Where shall we go tonight, honey? Hmm, what is my favorite type of sexual cuisine? What's yours?

Flour and garlic may be about the same in every restaurant's kitchen. But the dinners they serve can be as wildly different as the far-flung countries of the globe. Think about it: Tweezing up morsels of sushi between squared-off chopsticks while seated demurely on tatami mats; swilling hearty beer with sauerkraut in the din of a Bavarian Oktoberfest tent; lavishly dining on escargot and canard à la reine on the Champs-Elysées in Paris; devouring a juicy slab of beef and a baked potato at a Kansas City steakhouse.

Likewise, there are many sexual archetypes available to you to choose from in the bedroom. And there is your favorite, your "home-cooked" archetype, the one you feel most comfortable "inside of" when you make love. The one you know your way around. Everything flows smoothly and easily in that "me" archetype. We should add that this can change through time, circumstances, and with different partners.

But which one is it? Who are you in the majesty of your bedroom castle? And what is the full range of archetypes to choose from?

You're Invited to Dine

Try to identify your "home" sexual archetype. It is the one that:

- Gets your sexual juices flowing most effortlessly
- Has that comfortable "it's me" feeling; you know your way around
- Your body already "knows" about, there's no need to think your way into it
- Fills you with adoration and heartfelt lust for your partner

Here, we will describe nine sexual archetypes. One of them may be yours, your "home" archetype. Others may be familiar alternates for when you're in different moods. Some you may have never visited, or even ever imagined existed before. There is adventure here. Some you may not want to visit ever, but it's nice to know they're there. Perhaps a particular archetype is not your style at all, but it's your lover's favorite. You might want to try to understand that one better, to enjoy your partner more deliciously.

Whether you stay happily "home" in your one favorite sexual archetype, or travel adventurously among the full spectrum of archetypes, just dining on archetypal cuisine itself, instead of grabbing a quick bite to eat, can be enormously renewing and revitalizing for you and your relationships. The existence of a sexual archetypal realm is amazing enough. What a wonderful bonus it is that there is a cornucopia of sexual archetypes to choose from, and to share with your partner. This is a rich world indeed!

Sex, like dining, is an experience of the soul and the body, our heavenly palates soaring while our earthly hunger is sated. We don't just *think* about sexual archetypes, we *embody* them, too. We take them on, we drink them in, we imbibe them. From "inside" them we act in distinctive ways guided by their mythic content until they take us over in a kind of benign possession.

As you will see in the following chapters, every aspect of your sexual time together is brightly colored by these archetypes. They've been there all along, perhaps stealthily eluding your notice—and your command. For example, you flirt differently depending on which archetype you are embodying at a given moment.

Contrasting Sexual Archetypes

Let's look briefly at the first two sexual archetypes to see just how different they can be. Each of the nine has its unique character (we'll cover them all shortly), but let's start with these two to get a taste of their distinct flavors.

The Innocent *New to sex, playful, trusting, spontaneous*
The Adventurer *Daring, curious, fearless, explorative*

If you are playing out the Innocent, you might flirt with your partner in a simple, tentative, yet genuine manner. You might say something almost childlike, such as, "Can you come out and play today? Please. I'd love to hold your hand." From the Innocent, you might expect seemingly outrageous lines like, "Did you see my new silk panties? Aren't they pretty?" This come-on can slip right by as only mildly provocative. But the Innocent doesn't require an intense response. With its mild intensity, this archetype is a good place to build the trust necessary to allow you to venture later into more erotically charged archetypes.

Then again, it's quite a different matter if you're playing the Adventurer. Here, you embody a more daring persona. Talking about the very same underwear, you might challenge your partner: "I dare you to take off my panties with your teeth" or perhaps, "What's that you've got in your pocket, big boy?" You might also wear more provocative clothing like torn cutoffs or neon lipstick. Here you're raising the stakes a bit; turning up the heat a notch.

And that's just the *first two* of the nine archetypes described in this book. Already, you can see that not only are these two sexual archetypes quite distinctly different, but that there is a kind of natural flow or story line connecting them together, one to the other. The Innocent role is more like playing with matches while the Adventurer takes the next step of igniting the fire.

Your Mythic Journey

Even though you may live (and love) solely in a single favorite archetype, in fact, each is embedded in the larger context of the narrative flow of all nine sexual archetypes. Moreover, they follow a kind of mythic journey, reminiscent of Joseph Campbell's *Hero's Journey*, tracing out our universal sexuality. It is you in the mirror, *and* all of us collectively reflected as well.

Hence, this book is two books in one. This book is both a how-to lexicon of these nine archetypes, and a story of the odyssey of our collective sexual awakenings and return home. This book is a reference work and an epic story. The story is a journey of transformation, of deepening intimacy with yourself, with the characters that play out the drama of your inner lives.

Going from playing with matches on to igniting the fire, the point of the tale becomes clear: It must climax (as it were) in a roaring bonfire of heat and passion. That's the end-game. Right?

Well, our story does indeed go there. But, as it turns out, the bonfire is just the third of nine sexual archetypes! Where does it go from there? Aren't we "there"?

Where you go *after* the bonfire is, in a sense, the bigger theme of this book. The erotic soul of humans is vast indeed. It is perhaps far more than would ever have been required for mere biological procreation. Yet these archetypes stare at us, inviting us to fulfill the call of their sirens. And so this book is a dedication to our collective humanity, to surprise and wonder, to opening and expansion, to the infinite and lyrical character of the human spirit.

Shadows, Transformation, and Creativity

This is not to say that all of sex is upbeat and happy. All of us know of the tangles and darkness of relationships, the heartbreak of loss, the sadness of betrayal. These sexual archetypes also have their *Shadow* sides. These gloomy regions of the universe demand attention, too. And we will excavate some of this here as well. In so doing, you have a chance to heal yourself as never before. This approach is valuable in that you'll learn that your sexuality can transform you.

In the larger picture, your sexuality is the nuclear fire of your very creativity. Ignite your passion, your deep flowing lava, your molten core, and enliven your imagination. In a world desperate for renewal and peace, depleted from environmental destruction and war, we all need creativity more than ever. We all need creative, innovative minds to revitalize our world.

But you don't need to focus directly on renewing your creativity. That will happily happen on its own. Your task is to invite in the deities, call in the archetypes, and dance your dreams awake. This will unleash a river of creativity. But how to actually *do* that, to live out such a poetic vision? The short answer is step by step, jump in and try it, "fake it till you make it." Follow the practical exercises in this book. Suspend your disbelief. Let the magic come from nowhere. Begin with prose. Let the poetry of your soul awaken on its own.

Michelle and I listened as Dr. Oona began describing these amazing sexual archetypes. At first, I was a bit confused, but Michelle reminded me that it would all make sense when we started practicing them at home. Sounded like juicy fun to me. I was ready to jump into bed and get started right then!

But how to begin? Better keep listening to Oona so we get the whole road map first. Slowly, it started making more sense as things started fitting together into the bigger puzzle. It was like Oona gave us the TV Guide to all nine archetype channels.

Now I really wanted to know: What's Michelle's "home" archetype? What's mine? And what are other possibilities?

— Michael

Make yourselves comfortable. Pile up some soft fluffy feather pillows and snuggle up under a favorite cozy down comforter. Get ready to invite some new characters into the inner sanctum of your bedroom. Who will these new passionate playmates be? Who should be on the select invite list? Who will sing your heart songs when you make love and celebrate your bodily wonder with your lover? Who shall come to your sweet, daring ceremony?

None other than your very own sexual archetypes!

The world is teaming with archetypes, from Zeus to Madonna to Aphrodite. There are crowds of them. Fortunately, you'll only be inviting *sexual* archetypes to the party. And even so, we had to pare down our invite list to nine juicy main characters. Otherwise, we wouldn't have had a prayer of getting to know any of them. Still, if nine strangers showed up at a party, it might be hard to keep them all straight.

We'll be introducing our archetypes as characters in a vital story line. We'll bring them on stage one at a time. We'll get to know each character as well as we can. And then that character will make way for the next one, in a natural progression. We'll begin the story with our very first innocent sexual awakenings, and "test drive" our way through the characters. Each character, in turn, will add a splash of new color to your own sexual self-portrait. Hopefully, in the end, you will see a fuller, more magnificent me and us in the mirror.

After you've become familiar with all of the archetypes, the full troupe will be at your disposal for your encounters in the bedroom. Or not. When you desire their presence, any of them will be available to enhance your lovemaking. You will be able to pick and choose, at will, just the right persona in the whim of the moment. That's when it really gets fun! At first, you may be a bit awkward at "switching" your sexual personae at will. You may be a little slow at accessing just the right character in the heat of the moment. But practice makes perfect. And what a pleasure it is to practice in this arena! In due time, you'll learn to be quite spontaneous. Not to worry.

In the meantime, though, it's helpful—and easier—to get to know each archetype, one at a time, in a connected and meaningful manner. Along the way, you will encounter new challenges, and come face to face with new, perhaps unfamiliar, parts of yourself. The process may change you, as adventures into any uncharted psychic lands can do.

You may discover a wellspring of creativity hiding in the crevices between old habits. You may rekindle that artistic spark which crackled so fervently back in grade school a million years ago. You may find yourself painting new works of art with the brushes of your and your partner's bodies, and the watercolors of your imaginations. All of this can be ecstatically renewing. But most of all, the process will be just a whole lot of fun.

The Road Map

There is an irresistible movement inside each archetype. Archetypes aren't frozen. They're changing and they animate us with movement. There is also an unstoppable progression from one archetype to the next. And then *back around again.* We all start out young, gradually grow up—only to grow so mature, we're ready to open ourselves up to new possibilities with the innocence of a child. And back around again.

In a way, the nine sexual archetypes form a kind of circular road map of our sexual psyches. They lay out much of the rich territory you can visit in the bedroom. So, let's look at them on a map with compass points and directions. You can use this to keep your bearings when you're visiting the archetypes one by one in the following chapters.

This map also helps illustrate mutual relationships among the archetypes. This is important because when you're with your partner, you are not always in the same archetype as your partner. Partners often come to each other from different archetypal places. This is part of the fun. Sexual sparks can fly when disparate archetypes meet!

But we're getting ahead of ourselves. Let's look at the entire palette of archetypes. Then we'll be ready to examine each one in detail.

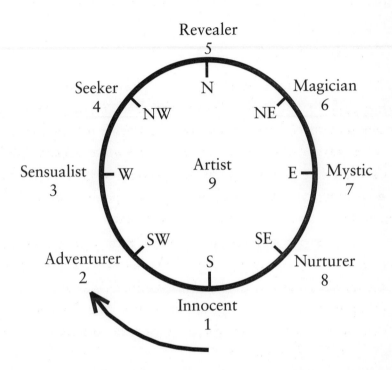

Breaking It All Down

Above, we've arranged the nine sexual archetypes with eight around the outside of the circle, and one last one, the Artist, in the center. This organization will make more sense later. For now, think of them as completely separate archetypes, each having its own enchantments. The plot will thicken....

Here's a snapshot of the unique characteristics for each sexual archetype:

The Innocent	*New to sex, playful, trusting, spontaneous*
The Adventurer	*Daring, curious, fearless, explorative*
The Sensualist	*Lustful, sizzling, physical, bold*
The Seeker	*Tantalizing, suspenseful, dramatic*
The Revealer	*Candid, ruthlessly honest, available, full of light*
The Magician	*Masterful, enchanted, knowledgeable, powerful*
The Mystic	*Intergalactic, spiritual, in tune with the universe*
The Nurturer	*Cozy, snuggled, savoring home-sweet-home*
The Artist	*Creative, versatile, improvisational, changeable*

Note that we *could* walk through the nine archetypes in any order. However, in this book, we will visit the archetypes beginning at the bottom with the Innocent, proceeding clockwise around to the Nurturer, then finally ending up in the center with the Artist.

As you will see, this order has the advantage that it describes the sort of mythic *Hero's Journey* storyline, reminiscent of Joseph Campbell's work. Taking this particular route, the archetypal puzzle pieces fit together quite nicely and memorably. Of course, you will have your own unique journey and may learn to love these archetypes in varying degrees, and in some other order. We've found that the order we employ is helpful for learning and explaining them. And around we go, not in a circle, but in a spiral of ever-deepening intimacy and self-knowing. This is the breathtaking, breath-giving rhythm of the universe.

THE ARCHETYPES IN FAST-FORWARD

To get started, here's a synopsis of the flow of the archetypes as one gives way to the next, moving around the wheel.

The archetypal journey begins with the lighthearted Innocent, segues to the explorative Adventurer, then turns up the erotic heat with the arrival of the salacious Sensualist. Next, the Seeker adds a cerebral, dramatic element of suspense, tension, and mystery to the sexual play.

The Revealer pauses to make sense of it all, to bring precious unspoken secrets to the light. Next, the Magician turns the attention to what needs to be healed, to help the lover overcome a hurdle or achieve a new level of growth. From there, you'll meet the cosmic Mystic, who opens the sexual realm up to the entire universe. Finally, you'll return home to the comfortable Nurturer for some renewing snuggling and rest, before you begin the journey all over again.

As a grand finale, when you feel fluent and adept with these eight archetypes, we'll explore a ninth archetype, the Artist, who is able to conduct all of the archetypes in a grand symphony of creative sexual expression.

Slowing the Pace

Yes, we know, that was quick. And maybe a little too high-level at this point. So, let's start over. This time, we'll take a specific example. Then we'll walk through the archetypes again more vividly.

Let's suppose you just bought some brand-new lacy silk underwear. You love them. You come home and you can't resist flirting a bit. Would your flirting look different depending on which of the nine sexual archetypes you're visiting? You guessed it. The answer is yes. Here's what you or your partner might say depending on which archetype you're "playing" at the moment:

The Innocent	*"Did you see my new silk panties? Aren't they cute?"*
The Adventurer	*"I dare you to take off my panties with your teeth."*
The Sensualist	*"Please touch my silk panties…Yes, right there, ooh…."*
The Seeker	*"I'll take my new silk panties off, but only if you beg me."*
The Revealer	*"I want to tell you a secret about my silky panties."*
The Magician	*"Let me show you how I want you to remove my silk panties."*
The Mystic	*"I shed my silk panties, opening my temple door to the universe."*
The Nurturer	*"Let me take off your panties so we can get ready for bed."*
The Artist	*"Panties or no panties the dance will go on."*

Here's a more whimsical example that contrasts our archetypes within another motif. Pretend you're in the Garden of Eden. Depending on the archetype, Adam and Eve's apple has a different spin:

The Innocent	*"That apple sure looks delicious."*

The Adventurer *"I dare you to bite into my apple."*

The Sensualist *"That apple is delicious, yum."*

The Seeker *"Where do you plan to put that apple?"*

The Revealer *"Oh, I get it, it's the apple of knowledge."*

The Magician *"I'd like to share this apple with you."*

The Mystic *"Through the apple, I enjoy the whole Garden."*

The Nurturer *"I baked you an apple pie."*

The Artist *"Let's grow apples."*

Hopefully, you're starting to get the hang of it, or at least a whiff of what's to come. Don't worry, we've got a full chapter on each archetype. With sexual archetypes, the best way to learn them is to *embody* them too. So plan to practice them —with your loved one, of course—in the safety and privacy of your bedroom.

You Are Innocent

Now it's time to put away the maps, compasses, and round diagrams. It's time to put away the Yellow Pages with its listings of *all possible*restaurants. Time to choose a single fine dining establishment—the alluring sexual delights of the Innocent.

And now that you've had a glance at the full suite of fine-dining choices, pause for a moment, and flush the rest of them out of your mind. Now dive into this first sexual archetype as if it were the only archetype on the entire planet. And dive into your partner as if she or he is the only other person you've ever met. Read, discuss, test drive, experiment, dress up in costumes, make mistakes, laugh. This is a how-to book. Let the pages get crinkled in the bedsheets while trying out some new possibility, some new alchemy of personae.

CHAPTER TWO

Playing with Matches

THE INNOCENT

*"The essential self is innocent,
and when it tastes its own innocence,
knows that it lives forever."*

— John Updike

We couldn't wait to get going. Dr. Oona had tantalized us with nine different ways to fly, spinning our minds like loose compass needles. I was ready to slow down, settle down, and just hang out with one of these sexual archetypes for a while.

I'd heard about archetypes in school. I even wrote a term paper on them once. But I had to admit, I still didn't totally understand what they are. Dr. Oona explained that archetypes are like airplanes. You can talk about them all you want, but until you fly in one, you can't relate to the sensation.

Dr. Oona told us to set the stage for the Innocent by going out to dinner together and pretending it was our very first date, as if we'd never met before. Mmm hmm! That was a fun night. By the time we got home, we were really in the mood to play out the Innocent archetype.

— Michelle

AND YOU?

We'll get back to Michelle and Michael in a moment. But first, what about you? Are you playful during sex? Do you like to feel utterly vulnerable? Do you like surprise, flirting, and touching? If this is your idea of fun, then you're in for a treat with the Innocent sexual archetype. If not, we invite you to explore the Innocent with the open mind and the open heart of an ingénue. Let's see what sublime pleasures are in store for you. Here are some situations and phrases that sum up this archetype:

- "Ooh, you've never touched me like that before. I love it!"
- That squeaky clean feeling of just getting out of the shower
- The unexpected tickle, the shudder, the wake-up kiss on the back of the neck
- Spontaneity: "Oh, I really don't know what's going to happen next."
- Sweetness, heartfelt caring, snuggling: "Hold me tight, pretty please."
- Surprise, wonder: "Hey, fancy meeting you here, sweetie!"
- Serendipity: "This is the perfect evening together—right out of the blue, too."
- No reasons: "Just 'cuz it would be fun. Let's just do it right now."
- Free-flowing, open-hearted emotions: laughter, tears, hugs, happiness
- And of course, naïve, wonderful, ingenuous, virginal innocence

When you're "inside" the Innocent archetype, you desire:

- Fun and ease
- Trust, heart connection, safety, empathy, love
- Relaxed time, no pressure, choices, no goals of orgasm
- Simplicity, just lying in a meadow or in bed all day
- Information: the ABCs of each other's sexuality, the basics, getting started
- Touch—all kinds, sexual and non-sexual
- Newly discovered feeling, caressing, skin-on-skin
- Wonderment at the whole rich world of pure, unedited sensation

What a way to start any sexual relationship—whether it's on a first date or it's a good-morning kiss of a 30-year marriage.

SEX ON THE "ISLAND OF YES"

To help you get a "feel" for a sexual archetype, sometimes it can be useful just to daydream on an image and pretend you're "there" for a few closed-eye minutes. To help you "see" the vista, we've put together an imaginary photo album of South Seas "Kodak moments," along with an endearing name for each one. We begin with the picture-perfect beaches of the *Innocent Island of Yes*.

We like to nickname it the Innocent Island of Yes because it has that blissful, nothing-can-go-wrong, timeless simplicity. It's how you might imagine yourself on a South Seas tropical island with succulent fruit glistening on the trees, tropical breezes fanning your skin-tingling body, and warm waters massaging your toes.

Sex in the Innocent

Now that you have an idea of how the Innocent operates, let's see how Michelle and Michael enjoyed "test driving" the Innocent the evening after their visit with Dr. Oona.

I can't believe I'm about to tell you how we made love last night. I would never have done that before. In a way, that's the fun thing about being in the Innocent archetype, everything is so easy. Making love is so fun. Even talking about it afterwards is fun.

Earlier in the evening, we'd playacted this spur-of-the-moment "wedding" together—just the two of us. I got dressed up in an old long, white, frilly dress from the back of my closet that we pretended was my wedding dress. After that, we headed right for our guest bedroom turned "penthouse" honeymoon suite. And we were the guests of honor. We were still dressed up and laughing. Michael undressed me, button by linen-covered button.

Michael was so sweet and gentle with me. I felt so deliciously vulnerable. When at last we snuggled under the cool, clean, starched sheets, our naked skin seemed smooth, wide open, and tingly—all of our skin, not just our genitals, drew us closer together. We hugged fully, body to body, and were mesmerized by candlelight. I was shuddering. After lying together, holding each other for awhile, Michael gently touched my bare shoulder with his fingertip. I thought I was going to come right then. I did, but not in an intense vaginal rush. It was more like an all-over body rush, electricity surging everywhere.

— Michelle

We'll continue with Michelle and Michael and their bedtime adventures in a few paragraphs, but first we're going to take a brief intermission to give you some how-to's so you can try out the Innocent role yourself. No fair just *reading* this book. We hope you jump in and take these archetypes for a spin. As you can see, sexuality in the Innocent archetype has this delicious flavor. It's:

- Playful, fun-loving, open to infinite possibilities, experimental
- Trusting, with no agendas, no expectations, no goals, no rights or wrongs
- Skin-to-skin, tuned into sensation, non-genital focused
- Perfect just the way you are, untouched body image, upbeat outlook
- Sweet, gentle, open-eyed, emotionally open, low intensity, open to surprise

It's sounds easy, and it is. But a few tidbits of advice can make it even easier—and help you avoid some small bumps in the road. Here are some quick tips:

- *Don't* talk about heavy issues; leave your old arguments at the door.
- *Don't* say "no." Say, "How about this instead, pretty please?"
- *Don't* fuss over what you should wear, do, or say.
- *Don't* be afraid: Have no fear, no holding back of your most respectful self.
- *Don't* board the "freight train to orgasm" (yes, we know it's tempting).

- *Do* listen to your heart's desires—and your partner's heart's desires. Keep the connection.
- *Do* come to your partner as if you're meeting for the very first time.
- *Do* focus on closeness and togetherness; spend time in never-never land.

- *Do* be attentive to you and your partner's raw skin—the smallest physical sensations.
- *Do* care for your partner. Ask, "Can I get you an extra pillow, sweetie?"
- *Do* pay attention to little details like sparkling eyes or a single strand of hair.
- *Do* venture into new territories; gather new insights; awaken to new revelations.
- *Do* unleash your laughter, play together, have fun, keep it light.
- *Do* enjoy your emotions: Let your tears flow like rivers.
- *Do* be enthusiastic. You are in a candy store. Try all the candy.

In the sexual arena, the Innocent is light, playful, open, genuine, joyful, connected, fragile, and vulnerable. Fun and sweetness are the motivations for this archetype. Anything too deep or too intense will be chased away by a joke or laughter, another interest, or even tears. The Innocent discharges intensity of any sort and gives curiosity, humor, and simplicity center stage.

Let's go through some specific facets of sex and see how they thrive in the Innocent archetype. This will help you see better if the Innocent is your home archetype—or if you'd like to travel here more often.

Flirting

The flirting of Innocents is genuine. In the Innocent, flirting style stems from a sense of being cute, irresistible, and desirable—and knowing it. The flirting is a game, but the Innocent doesn't know what to do with the energy that is engendered and is unconscious of its power. But who cares if it gets results? We just enjoy flashing our eyes, being a little naughty, and drinking from the other's presence. There is someone here right now who wants to spend this moment with you.

Of course, when you embody this archetype at a later age or stage of awareness, you will be absolutely aware of its power, and can just pretend not to be. You can still be Innocent at 80 years old, taking the experience of touching a new level of vulnerability. In any case, there is power in innocence, and depending on how innocent you are, your level of awareness will vary. Flirting from an Innocent place can be a shortcut to connecting more directly with another person in ways which would not normally be acceptable. In the Innocent archetype you can quickly dissipate any discomfort with a smile or a laugh.

Your Arousal

The source of your arousal in the Innocent is not so much your body as it is your heart. This is one of the most important roles the Innocent can play in deepening a relationship. In long-term relationships, or in older partners, when hormones are no longer the rocket fuel of your libido that they were at age twenty or thirty, a deepening of the heart connection is a way to keep arousal strong and fervent.

Your journey into the Innocent is not the time to discuss heavy issues in your relationship or things that make you un-comfortable. Nor is it the time to try to build a lot of erotic heat. The Innocent looks for information and fun rather than arousal and drama. Arousal that does happen is short-lived and staccato. Sometimes it will begin to build, then something might distract you and the turn-on might dissipate. That's fine. This is the signature of the Innocent.

You may get turned on in the Innocent. But not for long. Before you can get too aroused, you will probably be off on a new avenue of sensation. Let the erotic charge flow all over your body until they are as serene as the South Seas on a cloudless day.

Your Erotic Fire

In the Innocent, play is all-important. Cuddling and feeling loved and protected are as important as any other aspect. No need for grand passion at this point. Your passion will awaken later on the archetypal journey.

This "playful sex" can be a challenging task when old hurts and resentments have accumulated in a relationship. Many relationships allow the fire of erotic energy to leak away over time. As such, the Innocent can help rekindle the fire. Since this archetype allows arousal without the pressure of having to do anything with it, it is a good pathway for creating safety and healing—and renewal. It becomes a way to reconnect with erotic energy after it has seemingly slipped out of reach.

Your Relationship with Your Body

Your relationship with your body in the Innocent should be one of pride and discovery. Things are perfect just the way they are. There's no room for a negative body image, because the Innocent teaches us that nothing has yet been introduced to you that could cause such negativity. You may discover the pleasure of exhibitionism or the fun of displaying what you have to offer. Blessedly, the Innocent wears no armor. For the Innocent there is only the pure joy of the senses and the discovery of the physical experience. The Innocent is symbolically naked. (Of course, literally being naked is fine, too.)

Your Fantasies

Fantasies don't hold very much charge here, they are non-specific, mythic games just to "test drive" imagined experiences in our ever-fluid minds. You can leave them at any time. The titillation is enough. There's no agenda; no need to bring them to fruition. So, if you have been inhibited in sharing fantasies with your partner in the past, for fear that you might have to carry them out, the Innocent is a great safe haven to project these fanciful vignettes, dream-images, etc., on the silver screen of your bedroom wall—and munch on popcorn and laugh.

Meaning and Mastery

Changes and the emergence of new skills take place in steps. You will not master new skills right away. Try them out anyway, make mistakes, laugh, and try, try again. Any new archetype is clumsy at the beginning. Becoming comfortable in making mistakes is important to having a lively sex life. Making no mistakes means learning no new skills and reaching no new ecstatic victories. You have to experience the "beginner's mind" in growing and cultivating relationships.

All role possibilities are fluid in the Innocent. If you were to cross-dress as the opposite gender, for instance, it would be easy to become that gender because who you are is not "cast in stone." You can become whatever you like for a while—man, woman, or even the Queen of France. All play, including gender play, can open up exciting territory and new possibilities in your sexual relationships.

No need to seek grand, starry-eyed, cinematographic meaning at this point. For now, discovery and closeness provide quite enough meaning and focus of sex for the Innocent. Our experience is safety and comfort, feeling loved for our essential self. More meaning will appear later on our archetypal journey.

Your Orgasms

Since orgasms hold a special, well-deserved, exalted place in sex, we want to give this topic some extra attention. Let's first hear from Michelle and Michael and hear about their orgasms in the sweet embrace of the Innocent archetype.

I loved the gentle way Michael was stroking me, causing little baby orgasms all over my body. I didn't care if I came or not in the regular genital way. I was just riding the moment, feeling every hair on my naked arm that Michael softly skated over with his fingers, and feeling his wiggling toes intertwining with my toes. Sometimes I could feel my erotic energy start to build up a little, but then it would just scatter again, and then we'd be off in a different direction.

I'd always been used to going for the Big O, but this time it didn't matter. It was intense in a totally different way. When Michael slipped inside me, I gasped out loud. We grew totally silent. No moving, no thrusting, no nothing. Just listening to our genitals, like listening to a pin to drop. For the first time in my life, I slowed down enough to feel every tiny microscopic movement in my vagina. So did Michael. I never knew our genitals talked to each other so much. Neither of us came, but it was just as expansive, in a totally different way. Now that was truly making love!

— Michelle

Even orgasms in the Innocent have the fingerprints of this gentle archetype. For many people, these are brand new, undiscovered kinds of orgasms.

Here's a brief glance at Innocent orgasms:

- Full-bodied, ebbs and flows of sensation everywhere, skin-centered
- Low-intensity, low-pressure, sensuous, easygoing, no push for insertion
- No need for ejaculation or "Big O" explosions—or even an erection
- Stillness is common, as if you can hear a pin drop, even during intercourse
- Maintaining eye-to-eye connection even at moments of high pleasure
- "Listening" through your skin, your whole bodies, even through your genitals
- Talking, laughing, crying, joking anytime (remember: no rights or wrongs!)

The Innocent plays with sex just because it feels good, emotionally and physically. This archetype is not ready to commit to a lot of steamy passion. The Innocent is not geared towards orgasm (even though it may happen). The Innocent's focus is on *connection* rather than the Big O. The lack of intensity can even make it difficult for couples in this archetype to reach orgasm when they wish to. That's OK. However, in the quietude of the Innocent, you can discover those thousands of small, shuddering, rippling sensations which can wash over you at any time. These are also orgasms. Enjoy them. Savor them.

The Innocent can be a place where you discover orgasms that are not purely genital. These are more full-body "baby orgasms" like rippling waves in a calm alpine lake. As small as they might be, these orgasms are very important. They are the "beginning of the alphabet" of orgasms. In other archetypes, we will learn more of this "alphabet."

Many men discover here that orgasm does not necessarily equal ejaculation. Women can discover different kinds of orgasms, too. Here we can shift from goal-oriented sex, to basking for hours in the ecstasy of merging into oceanic bliss. The smallest muscle movement, even a word or an image, can set us pulsating. This can be fantastic training for more intense full-body sexuality later on in other archetypes.

We don't normally think of full intercourse within this archetype, but gentle penetration can be a sublime experience of "sharing the silence." Instead of wild thrusting, try hardly moving at all—almost like holding your breaths together— meditating in the "sacred temple" of the vagina. Just listen to your genitals. They have a lot to say. If you do this and can stay in the Innocent archetype, your sensations can be hyper-amplified. The smallest nuance can send either or both of you into a mini-orgasm. Then go back to golden silence. In the chapter on the Mystic archetype, you will learn how to maintain this level of ecstasy for blissful hours, then perhaps shift to a higher energy archetype for a grand finale. Or not.

The Journey of the Sexual Archetypes: The Beginning

As we've seen, the Innocent is a perfect place to begin, because it's about beginnings itself. The Innocent captures that wonderful feeling of "this has never happened before," of freshness, surprise, wonder—even if we've actually done it a million times before.

This open-hearted, playful curiosity is the sacred domain of the Innocent. If you want to enter the Innocent, call up that eight-year-old part of yourself who could leap into a swimming pool—or into life—without even dipping your toes in first. Cold? No problem. All the more tantalizing!

The Innocent is like that. Life is so safe and easy, there's no need to think first. Just play. There's no agenda. Let's just have some fun—in the pool, under the table, in the bedroom. You're not going anywhere; treat today like a lazy summer afternoon that lasts forever. Each sensation is new, as if it's never happened before. Just try things out, come what may, recognize each moment and its beauty.

This is the time of new beginnings and awakenings. Our hero and heroine are just embarking on their journey. Everything is bright and shiny and safe. It's the territory of the virgin, of Peter Pan, of the inner child. It's a time of discovery and possibility. There is no commitment to follow through on any thread of discovery. In fact, there's no need for it. It's simply a time to play, to show off, to be seen. When we're within the Innocent, the world is ours.

The first task is the integration of the heart. In our primal hearts, we are born into the intimate knowledge that trust is possible, that others truly care about us, that we are loved, that all is well in the world. This is home at its most comfortable.

If your natal home was not so cheery, not imbued with happy, home-sweet-home sweetness, then, surprisingly enough, this is your lucky day! This Innocent archetypal real-estate is the perfect place to build such a space with your partner in your adult life. You may shed tears for yourself here, but this is no time to get paralyzed by your childhood losses—or any other losses. With few exceptions, we can all learn to access this starting point in our archetypal epic journey.

The Innocent is an ideal "first archetype" because it is concerned with the safety and connection between partners. Amidst the open-hearted fun, two lovers are forging a deep bond with each other. When we are close and deeply connected, opening to new territory feels exciting because the bond will carry over and the trust is solid. This depth of closeness is what makes us feel safe enough to play with the tension we'll encounter in other archetypes.

With great innocence, we can touch taboos and come away unscathed. The shock of breaking a taboo is protected by laughter. Sex performer Annie Sprinkle uses innocence as a vehicle to deliver the most outrageous material about sexuality on stage. She displays her cervix to her audience in complete innocence. In innocence we cannot be perverted. At its best, the Innocent has not yet met the Shadow, so there is no shame or judgment.

For some, the Innocent may seem brand new. However, most of us have already encountered the Innocent in other contexts. They may not be sexual per se, but they do convey the underlying themes well, and as such, can be inspirational.

The Innocent archetype is like Adam and Eve in the Garden of Eden—before eating the apple. Princess Di projected an Innocent archetype. Even sexy Marilyn Monroe expressed it in her flirtations. Hugh Grant is typecast frequently in this role, as in the movie *Sirens*. Another movie which conveys the Innocent well is *Forrest Gump*, as well as the protagonist in *Titanic*. Peter Sellers's beautiful movie *Being There* also captures this archetype well, as does George, the main character in Steinbeck's *Of Mice and Men*. We get glimpses of the Innocent more often than we might imagine.

How to Get Started

Maybe you're reading this chapter together snuggled in your bed together. Perhaps you're thinking that you'd love to play in the sandbox of the Innocent, but you can't figure out how to get the ball rolling with your partner.

So far in this chapter, we saw Michelle and Michael at Dr. Oona's office, and then we skipped to their Innocent sexual play at home, but how did they get into that playful, juicy frame of mind? How did they kick start the Innocent archetype? Here, we will try to fill in the gap and show you how you they got started, and how you might initiate the same scenario.

CREATING THE MOOD

We sometimes call this the "Theater of the Bedroom," although, as you'll see here, much of the "theater" happens well *outside* the bedroom. It's "theater" but don't think scripts and contrived acting. Nevertheless, do think of, improvisation, and imagination. You might even need to ham it up a bit to get into the mood. After that, just be your free-flowing, natural self.

Let's see how Michael and Michelle set the stage for their adventure into the Innocent.

When Dr. Oona suggested we go out to dinner and act like it was our very first date, I thought she was out of her mind. I had no idea how to pretend to be something I'm not. Michelle has a lot of actress in her, but me, I'm just a regular guy, not too big on imagination.

Michelle practically had to drag me over to this hip hamburger hideaway across town. Then she made me want to crawl under the table when she told the waitress we'd just met on a park bench half an hour ago, but that I seemed like a nice guy.

Then, something strange happened. I don't understand it. But all of a sudden, I started to get into it. It was like something clicked inside me. Somebody hit the "on" switch. Electricity started to buzz.

I blurted out, "Hey cutie, wanna get a milkshake with two straws and sip together?" She giggled—exactly like she really did on our actual first date! I loved it. When we got the shake we sucked on the straws with our faces about two inches apart, making eyes at each *other. And then when she started playing footsies with me, I footsied her back, and then I started laughing and couldn't stop.*

I had no idea I could play-act like that. More than that, I was totally loving it, and was feeling closer to Michelle than I had in years.

— Michael

Things to remember when inviting in the Innocent:

- Go into that "let's pretend" place which was so easy as a child.
- Put your inhibitions and self-image criticisms and judgments away.
- Enjoy and delight in your embarrassments.
- Fly on the magic carpet of your imagination, travel to magic fairylands.
- Look at your partner and really believe that you're on a first date, now!
- "Think lovely thoughts," as Peter Pan and Tinkerbell would say.
- Do something which you haven't done before, or don't normally do.
- Go ahead and ad-lib, as if you're doing improv theater.
- Look at your partner, pay sweet attention, keep the connection.
- Let yourself be blown away that you're actually alive in this moment!
- Be innocently outrageous, mildly provocative, curious yet gentle.

Sometimes, the hardest part of enjoying sexual archetypes is just getting started. How do we flip the "on" switch for a particular archetype? Sure, once you get used to them and the archetypes become a natural, regular part of your sexual vocabulary, the switching can become automatic. But until then, it's often very helpful to use little tricks like first-date games or costumes to "kick start" an archetype.

But don't worry, costumes are like bicycle training wheels: You mostly need them to get started. You might be a little wobbly at first. However, once you've got the knack, you can leave the training wheels behind in the garage, and your costumes in the closet. (Actually, unlike training wheels, costumes can continue to be fun to bring back out of the closet occasionally! But more on that later.)

As Michael and Michelle learned, a great way to invite the Innocent archetype into your midst is to play-act a first-time activity together. Going out to dinner on a pretend first date is a perfect way to climb inside the Innocent archetype. Other ways to get it going are to imagine yourselves in the mood of virginity, innocence, never done this before, tentativeness, maybe with a dash of awkwardness.

Even though you might be 42, living in a suburban ranch house with Lassie barking out back, for this evening you can pretend you're a virginal, sweet, never-done-it-before teen, on your way to the senior prom. "Oh my god, he's picking me up in half an hour. What will I wear?" Or, "I think she might have a crush on me. I'm so nervous. Um, honey, can I smell that rose on your lapel?"

Creating the Space

Let's return to Michelle and Michael and see where their "first date" takes them.

♂ *When we got home from our first date, Michelle was still giggling like a teenager. Neither of us wanted to stop. We hardly skipped a beat, pausing quickly just to turn off the phone, latch the door, and pull down the shades. Then we dove into the closet, rummaging around looking for clothes to keep the gaiety going. Some other time, I might have felt inhibited or shy, but this night, we felt free to follow our fancies wherever they took us.*

— Michael

Archetypes are powerful, yet jealous creatures. They don't like to share their realms with earthly distractions. Be sure to honor the archetypes—and yourselves—by paying attention to "creating the space." Even though the mood of the Innocent is spontaneous, take a few minutes ahead of time to carefully plan an uninterrupted evening together. Turn off the phone. Lock the door. Give yourselves the privacy you so well deserve. Seal off the world, and protect your most tender intimate moments from the harsh daylight of public scrutiny, exposure, and interruptions.

The "space" where you live out the archetypes is critically important. Like an oven, an enclosed, defined space enables a higher temperature. It will hold and contain you, without confining you. In fact, a strong container makes more freedom of expression possible, more of your infinite imaginations welcome, more parts of you will be invited to play.

For the Innocent, spaces and boundaries are for safety, so your heart can open or move to a deeper level. The Innocent awakens within strong boundaries, yet is not even conscious of the extent of the boundaries.

Costumes and Props

Even if you're not an actress or an actor, don't miss out on costumes. It's just astonishing how powerful costumes can be in instantly changing the way people feel inside themselves. For some people, it feels like a brain transplant. Perhaps you also feel like a new person with a new set of clothes.

Our closet was stuffed full of old clothes and tons of fun stuff. Michelle found an embroidered white dress that reminded her of her mom's wedding dress, and put it on. She looked 22. I put on a pair of cutoffs. In the mood we were in, just about anything could work. I especially liked the sweet, innocent look. All that white lace on Michelle made her look almost virginal. It made me feel kind of shy and inexperienced, too, but ready to experiment nonetheless.

— Michael

As you prepare to meet the Innocent, think about dressing up for a first date. Wear almost embarrassingly innocent costumes, clothing that makes you feel vulnerable, sweet, precious, cute, and lovable. Think: wedding-night white, or the ripped T-shirt you wore to summer camp. You could choose to dress as your own young child-self or as the child you always wanted to be. Actually, almost anything can be a prop for the Innocent. Being unprepared is the key, because there is no preconception of what must be prepared for. Accordingly, an intentional gathering up of toys or of scene-setting will wait for later archetypal enactments.

In the Innocent archetype, lovers become grade-school sweethearts again. You can travel back to that carefree, first-time feeling, even with a long-time mate, and discover your partner for the first time again, in ways you hadn't imagined. It is the place to become a virgin again, opening up a part of yourself that you had long since forgotten.

The things you do to call forth the Innocent archetype needn't be complicated. In fact, they mustn't be. To begin, you could say, "I have a crush on you..." or "I'll show you mine if you'll show me yours." Think about what activities feel safe to you. You could rock the other in your arms, wash each other's feet, cuddle, stroke each other's hair, play games. Maybe you play-act that you have found a pile of erotic magazines under your parents' bed. You could pretend you've never met and make a date on the phone—have a conversation to begin to discover one another. Choose what you will wear on your date.

It can also be helpful to make an agreement beforehand not to have sex or any orgasm-oriented activity. This is your first time. Create it the way you would have liked it to be. Later on, say, after a day of letting things settle, take time to talk about the experience. Sharing your differing points of view and discoveries will help you to prepare for your next ceremony.

EMOTIONS

Michelle looked so demure in her mom's crinkly old white wedding dress, and I felt as if I was back at summer camp in my cutoffs. Then she pulled out a toy stethoscope. We were about to play doctor, when we got distracted fumbling with a million buttons on the wedding dress, and we decided to have a wedding right then instead.

We put on a CD of Wagner's "Wedding March," looked into each others' wet eyes and gently traded rings. Even I thought it was very sweet. Then we thought, oh, let's have a honeymoon night together— tonight. "Do you need help with those buttons, honey?" I really did feel a little modest, like somehow I really believed in that moment that we'd never undressed together before. That was hot.

— Michael

When you're in the Innocent archetype, emotions flow easily and swiftly—lots of emotions. Like babies, you might cry one minute, be giggling the next minute, and be back in a serious mood in a third minute—or almost that fast. There's no need for continuity of emotion or train of thought. That's okay. One thing leads to another, and another, like the streams of consciousness Virginia Woolf portrays in her novels.

For example, you might be lying on your backs in a meadow enjoying a warm summer day, looking at the white puffy clouds racing by. Perhaps, you quietly reach over and touch your lover's inner arm, electrifying her whole body. Perhaps suddenly, you're getting a little turned on, wanting to snuggle a bit closer on your blanket. But, before you can amp up the energy another notch, you notice a cloud that looks like a cross between a giraffe and an elephant. You both see it. You both laugh. And completely forget that you were getting aroused just a few moments earlier.

When you're within the Innocent, you might "strike matches" just to see what they can do. You can stare at the small flickering flame and feel the new, unexpected changes of your nascent passion. It's fine to play with matches, but you don't need to build big erotic fires—not just yet, and not in this archetype. Stay tuned for that later.

In the Innocent, you can light matches, but often they fizzle out, like striking a match on a windy day. And that's fine. No fire is needed. If one starts, there's no need to keep it going. The match play itself can keep you happily occupied, involved with each other, and connected in a meaningful way. No burdens, no cares. It's just whatever happens, happens.

While there is little continuity of emotions in the Innocent, in a larger sense, there is one overriding, very continuous feeling—the feeling of trust and safety. You can know your partner will never hurt you here, cares deeply for you, is yours totally—and this sense is so sure, you don't even need to say it out loud. It's understood, and as such, it is much more powerful than any spoken promises could ever be. Trust is in the very fabric of this archetype. So, the Innocent is a great place to rekindle lost trust, to repair old betrayals, refurbish tattered relationships, drink from the fountain of happily-ever-after youth. The Innocent is a good place for you to "meet" each other again, and even to fall in love again. The rest of our archetypal journey will benefit from any trust established and deepened here in the playful Innocent.

The Shadow

With all the playfulness of the Innocent, we don't want to give you the wrong impression: that life under the spell of the Innocent is all sunshine and happiness. Even in the Innocent, there can be sadness, loss, and betrayal. This is the Shadow side of the Innocent archetype. Michael and Michelle have a close brush with this disconnected, unhappy, "cloudy" side of the Innocent themselves.

I was so glad Dr. Oona had warned us about what she called the "Shadow" or dark side of the Innocent archetype. It made us aware that the Innocent is not just all sunshine and kissing. I would have thought that being Innocent, you could do just about anything you wanted and everything would go great, no matter what. But there really are bumps in the road. And if I hadn't been looking out for them, I'm sure I would have steered right into a couple of big ones.

The night of our "first date," I got really into putting on my costume and mugging for the mirror. When I got just so, just perfect, I turned to Michael to show off how beautiful I looked. Michael was combing his hair at the time, and hardly noticed me. I wanted him to admire me. I waited. Nothing. Then, I felt this wave of anger and hurt wash through me. I almost burst out saying, "You never pay attention to me. You're so self-centered." But fortunately I realized I was trying to use Michael to help me feel good about myself.

Later in the evening, I hit another, bigger speed bump. In the slow-motion mood of the Innocent, I was luxuriating on Michael's intimate stroking of my inner thighs. I was drinking in the pleasure without thinking a whit about anything else or anyone else. I was really just a cheap, selfish pleasure slut. Like pure pleasure was somehow not OK. But then I remembered that there are no rights and wrongs in the Innocent.

At that point our togetherness cooled down a couple of degrees. It was a big lesson for me. I gave Michael a big wet kiss and met his eyes. The second time, I ran my finger up his shorts for good measure. In a flash, we were back in sync.

— Michelle

Shadows, in the psychological sense, can be deep and mysterious, and hard for us to grasp. This is because your Shadow, by its very nature, will be hidden from you. And yet, your Shadow can affect your life deeply, especially within your relationships and love lives. There is much gold to be mined in dem thar hills. A major part of many people's journey to self-insight is unearthing their Shadows in an attempt to become more conscious of their own will and deeper intentions, so we will attempt to look at the Shadow sides of all of our nine archetypes.

The Shadow side of the Innocent is its avoidance of inner conflict, as well as lack of mature person-to-person connection —and corresponding lack of depth. The Innocent is a wonderfully fun archetype to visit again and again, but it's not a license for self-absorption. If we get engulfed in only the pure silly playfulness of this archetype, we'll be unable to continue on the journey of discovery. We will feel malnourished on our Mythic Journey.

But don't confuse love of pure pleasure with self-absorption, either. Practice being present to yourself and your partner. You can do both. There is no inherent conflict here. If there is a conflict, it may be an inner conflict over the rightful place of pleasure in your life; over what you truly deserve.

The Shadow of the Innocent is exemplified in the Peter Pan Syndrome, the boy who wouldn't grow up. As such, a relationship with another person who is confined to the Shadow side of the Innocent archetype can be frustratingly superficial due to the person's fleeting, fragmentary character and short attention span. The short charge-discharge cycles can keep you from going deep with this kind of lover. He or she is easily distracted and cannot sustain long moments of deep connection. Many people stay in that archetype as a way to avoid experiencing conflicts that awaken with a stronger erotic charge.

When both partners in a relationship live primarily in the Innocent archetype, they might have a lot of easy fun, but when difficulties arise, they can become two hurt, out-of-control children with no one to hold the space for healing. Boundaries that work must include safety and unattachment to erotic outcomes.

Any emotions that surface should be given the space to run their course without judgment. Great sensitivity should be present in the case of a wounded Innocent, who requires nurturing support. Save edgy activities for another time—and another archetype.

In order to get more clarity on this Shadow theme, let's go backstage for a few paragraphs, and look at this Shadow theme from a sex therapist's perspective. Please excuse some of the jargon. Hopefully this "shop talk" will provide another level of insight into the Innocent's Shadow for many of our readers.

A lot of people who are sexually and emotionally wounded live in the dark side of the Innocent archetype. The bedrooms of our society are filled with so-called wounded inner children acting out. A common misuse of energy in this archetype is to use sex to get validation, love, and attention to fill up the narcissistic hole of the wounded child. This creates a push-pull dynamic for someone who is needing to feel loved and validated, but who is not really ready to be present and available for an intimate sexual encounter. Such individuals can disassociate sex from their emotions because they continually attempt sex for the "wrong" reasons.

Or more amazingly, some people even disassociate sex from their own physical bodies, desperately wanting to believe that sex is purely spiritual only—no messy physicality besmirching this heavenly realm! Childhood sexual trauma can often be the source of this disassociation. The trauma may be unwanted sexual advances—adult-style sex forced on them at too early an age. Or less often recognized, it can be too little childhood-style innocent sex, caused by aggressive suppression of self-pleasuring, masturbation, sexual play, etc., by adults. Either way, the Innocent is often rudely chased into hiding by adults. Not surprisingly, the media is obsessed with the more sensational former. But the latter suppression of childhood sex play is no doubt far more common, verging on epidemic in America. Therapists probably routinely confuse the former with this far more common way of people losing their connection with the Innocent.

LESSONS

When I caught myself staring at my show-off self in front of the mirror and ignoring Michael, it was like someone showed me a wide-screen movie of all the times I've spaced out, caring more about me than Michael. Later when I had that wave of guilt about pigging out on my own pleasure, I realized I didn't care enough about myself either.

I remembered a flood of really painful times when Michael ignored me over the years, or said really inconsiderate things. I'd stopped trusting Michael. And stopped wanting to feel deeply, feel from deep inside my body.

But this time something shifted inside me. That mirror helped me empathize more with Michael. It helped me accept myself more, too.

Mix those new insights together with surrendering to each other (and ourselves) tonight—and lots of those old wounds seemed to just evaporate.

— Michelle

Fortunately, there is good news for those people and couples ensnared by conflict, up past two A.M., bathed in the tears and drowning in the sticky tar pits of "but you said," "but I didn't mean it that way," etc.

The Innocent is an ideal archetype for healing sexual and emotional wounds, because every experience can be remolded, re-created, remade anew. There is an opportunity for a grand "makeover," to re-experience (formerly) painful events in new-found comfort and safety. This is the ancient concept of the Jubilee year where all debts are forgiven and we can all move on equally unencumbered.

Your Turn

So go ahead, and try your own version of the Innocent. Yours won't be quite the same as Michelle and Michael's version. Archetypes are very personal. And you are unique. You may be the same sex or different sex from your partner. You might not like milkshakes. There may even be more than two of you. There are tons of possibilities. But whatever you do together, if you can find your own sweet playful sanctum deeply connected with each other, you will discover realms which the deities have pre-pared for you, cave walls painted with the most splendid tableaux of the soul, and anointed with the nourishing waters of true love.

Here are a few ideas to get you going. Try imagining you are:

- On a first date
- At your wedding
- Going for a picnic in the park
- Playing doctor, etc.
- Off to senior prom night
- Being pleasured while actually pleasuring yourself
- A virgin, or single, or you haven't had sex for years
- Nervous about your "first time"
- Holding, hugging, being playful

♀ *What a honeymoon evening that was! It capped off a pretty amazing day. In the midst of it, sometimes Michael and I would just stop and stare at each other—our eyes meeting together like they had earlier in the evening over milkshakes, and then again later that night in that amazing wedding ceremony which came out of nowhere.*

I can't figure out why such silly play made me feel so connected to Michael. All those heavy dead-end conversations we'd had over the past year about our "relationship" were a total waste of time compared to one sensational evening of just playing together.

Trust is a great aphrodisiac, too. Not like giant fireworks, but so sweet and so together. We've just started touring these archetypes, and already, I feel like we've been showered by so many gifts.

— Michelle

Onward

A journey into the Innocent has offered us the gift of heartfelt openness, intimacy, and connection. Genuine openness, coupled with curiosity and connection, makes solid ground for exploration. In this state of pure being, one can stand totally naked before another, knowing that this nakedness is safe and sacred. It is the gift of the Innocent to be able to open up to new emotional experiences, to find oneself on new ground, naked for the first time again. A deeper meaning of the word virgin is "possessing the power to renew innocence." The Innocent has that power.

CHAPTER THREE

Igniting the Fire

THE ADVENTURER

"Follow Him through the Land of Unlikeness;
You will see rare beasts, and have unique adventures."
— W. H. Auden, *For the Time Being*

Michelle and I didn't want to leave the Innocent. We called it our little Island of Yes, a tropical Eden-like paradise where the only word you needed to know was "Yes."

Still, in spite of how much I liked the Innocent and how close Michelle and I had grown there, I was curious to discover new adventures beyond the horizon—and to discover my "home" archetype.

We knew we would enjoy sex a lot more when we fine-tuned our yes's and no's a bit, and were more clear about what got us hot and what cooled us down.

Dr. Oona told us to dream up some outrageous costumes, head out somewhere that might push our buttons a bit, and repeat the mantra "I dare you" to each other. I've always wanted Michelle to be a little more adventurous, so I was immediately on board. Michelle saw the glint in my eyes and just smiled. I wonder what she was thinking.

— Michael

We also wonder what Michelle was thinking. But we'll get back to Michael and Michelle after turning the flashlight in your direction for a few pages.

Are you an "edge walker?" Do you like to push the limits? Can you find that secret side of you that is just a little bit defiant? Do you think what society says about sex is, well, just plain dumb? Do you want to crank up the heat on your sex life a notch? Do you yearn to break out of the mold and get wild for a change?

Whether or not you've fully developed your adventurous side around sexuality, we invite you to—nay, we *dare* you to —run with the Adventurer archetype right now.

Let's look at some quotes that capture the essence of this second electric sexual archetype:

- "Ooh, baby, you've got an animal glint in your eyes. I smell danger."
- "I'm really not sure if I'd like that. Let's try it anyway. Go for it."
- "I'm curious, what's your most outrageous fantasy?"
- "My mommy told me not to do that in bed."
- "Me, afraid? Hello, I don't think so. Read my ripped T-shirt: No Fear!"
- "I like fast cars. And I like you that way too!"
- "No. Yes. I mean no. No wait, I mean yes."

Don't worry if you're not sure what you like and what you don't like. The Adventurer is where you will tune your tastes. It's your laboratory to find out where the steam is, and where the cold spots reside in your sex life.

When you're "inside" the Adventurer archetype, you want:

- Thrills, excitement, uncertainty, danger, juice, turn-ons, to "up the ante"

- Sparks flashing out of your eyes—and your partner's eyes
- No limits, no responsibilities, no cares, no plans
- Surprise mixed with a wee bit of shock
- A wild sense of freedom and exploration
- To drive over taboos, like an SUV crushing a bottle
- To be set free like an animal returned to the wild
- To be flamboyantly sexual and untamed—
  even promiscuous
- New information, to know what's really going on in
  your partner—and you
- To be touched in a slightly aggressive way, but always
  with love behind it

If your relationship has suffered from the "same-old" syndrome, or if sex has been getting a bit routine, the Adventurer may be just the tonic for you. The Adventurer may or may not be your "home" archetype. But even if it's not, the Adventurer can be a great place to rouse some excitement in your relationship.

So, let loose, and remember, like the Innocent, there are no rights and wrongs in Adventureland. Indiana Jones would never have found the Holy Grail if he'd been fussing over his table manners. While you're here, give yourself well-deserved time off from your normal predictable patterns and "mature" decorum. And enjoy!

SEX NEAR THE "REEFS OF DANGER"

Last chapter we hoped to give you a feel for the Innocent by sharing Island of Yes snapshots from our album. We have photos for the Adventurer archetype, too. Here is the second picture for you to daydream over.

Like the Innocent, we have a South Seas nickname for the Adventurer: the Reefs of Danger. To get a sense for the Adventurer, try imagining this: You've been basking in the sun on the Island of Yes for many languid days, occasionally staring off over the blue Pacific Ocean toward the hazy horizon, wondering what it's like out there.

One day, you can't resist your curiosity any longer. You and your partner put in your dugout canoe, and paddle out beyond the edge of your little intimate lagoon, out to uncharted waters. Just then, a squall comes up and drives you perilously close to a dangerous reef. In the same moment, you are scared—but very excited, too. You pump your oars double-time to avoid the rough coral and jagged rocks. In the midst of the frenzy you notice you haven't felt this alive in years!

When, at last, you tumble back onto your beach, you hug each other and rejoice in returning home safely. Then you notice something: a new glint, a never-before-seen intensity, a stronger spirit in your partner's eyes. You make love right then and there, as never before.

Sex in the Adventurer

Let's return to Michelle and Michael and see if they encountered some excitement. As we will learn later, they followed Dr. Oona's advice and had a very adventure-filled afternoon. We now rejoin them as they arrive home.

When we walked in the front door, our house seemed oddly much bigger, almost unfamiliar as if it had changed while we were having our naughty adventures in the park.

This time it was my turn. Without missing a beat, I unzipped Michelle's dress. She just stood there and let it fall on the living room floor. I still can't believe she wasn't wearing any panties.

She turned the tables and ripped off my clothes and pushed me down on the couch, face down. I could feel the rough corduroy of the cushions on my naked thighs as she spread my legs and skimmed her fingers over my derrière. She'd made playfully rude comments about my cute ass many times before, when she'd snuck peeks of me in the shower, but this was the first time she'd dared to linger there with her probing fingers.

I thought, I can't believe she's doing this. This is so totally off-limits. Then she touched an especially sensitive area and my mind went blank. Shorted out. No, wait, don't do that, I was about to scream out. But at the same time, I desperately wanted her to continue. I wondered where she'd learned to do that. And at the same time, I didn't care.

Michelle turned me over and slipped me inside her. My mind was washed in white radiance, and my eyes saw an expanding purple dome. In the little fragments of consciousness I had left, I was blown away that our sex had grown beyond our genitals to something far bigger.

— Michael

Sexuality in the Adventurer has a real tang to it. There probably should be a Surgeon General's warning on the outside wrapper of the Adventurer. It can:

- Break old patterns, replacing them with new, untested possibilities
- Challenge your sense of propriety; of being a good girl or a good boy
- Confuse you, wonder if what you've always believed is right anymore
- Reconnect you to the sense of excitement and possibilities in your life

- Amaze you, re-energize you, renew your relationship
- Expand your horizons, open up newfound creativity in yourself
- Clean up your psyche, clear away useless, obsolete patterns
- Turn you on in new ways and add more excitement to your sex life

This may sound harder than it really is. You'll get it. Here are some tips to help make things go even smoother:

- *Don't* panic. Your partner loves you and really wants this to be fun.
- *Don't* worry about losing yourself and your values; they are strong.
- *Don't* be concerned about getting hooked on pleasure, or about being insatiable
- *Don't* hold back your fantasies; some may be surprising and shocking, and that's okay.
- *Don't* be critical or consider yourself a pervert; you're just exploring your imagination.
- *Don't* get caught up in a particular idea, or plan, or fantasy.
- *Don't* be afraid to tell off-color jokes, laugh at sacred cows, or call a spade a spade.
- *Don't* freeze up, just stay relaxed and stay in your emotions.
- *Don't* use the words "yes" or "no" for a while; use other more imaginative words.
- *Don't* forget to love, touch, and adore your partner, and enjoy yourself too.

- *Do* listen to your body's deepest, most secret desires—and your partner's desires.
- *Do* cultivate that sense of wild teenage abandon.
- *Do* take risks, try new things, touch new places, experiment with each other.
- *Do* be provocative, daring, wild-eyed, and iconoclastic.
- *Do* stay spontaneous, be in the moment, ad-lib, improvise.
- *Do* talk about what's going on inside of you while you're feeling it.
- *Do* love, touch, and shower your partner with adoration.

Remember, the big idea behind the Adventurer is to find out what you like and don't like, what turns you on and what lowers the temperature, how far you can go, where the edges of your sexuality reside. And where are your partner's edges? Remember to stay conscious and connected to your partner. Don't get carried away with dares and double-dares. There's a lot to be learned in the Adventurer about your own sexual turn-ons. That's why we turn to arousal next.

Your Arousal

Much of the focus of the Adventurer is on arousal and excitement. From discovering a new orifice, a new level of subtlety, or a different sexual orientation, the Adventurer tests preferences and limits, gathering information about what truly arouses you. The Adventurer can help you "customize" your unique sexuality.

In the Adventurer, you can discover which images hold charges; which experiences have erotic interest. There is a fresh quality to the erotic, a sense of amazement that pushes the edges of eroticism and energizes a whole range of sexuality. Like the forbidden (yet alluring) apple in the Garden of Eden, once you take a bite, nothing will ever be the same again.

Your Body

In the Adventurer, your body and your psyche will have the opportunity to experience a new level of sexual energy, to hold *more* sexual tension.

In the Adventurer, there is the invitation to touch and experience the many possibilities that exist in sexuality, in our body and in human relationships. Open the doors, try things out and see if they interest you—think about them later. Nothing is cast in concrete. In the Adventurer, the body is the laboratory of experimentation. The body is not imprinted yet, so there's plenty of room for new discoveries. Suspend your disbeliefs. Let your body be your teacher. It knows.

Your Erotic Fire

The Adventurer's sexual experiences are about fun and variety. How many orgasms can I get? How far can I jerk off? I dare you to go to a business meeting with no underwear. How do I get to a higher level of arousal? What about sex toys and other unusual things? I want to try them.

The variety and range of the Adventurer sexuality stems from the desire to try out all possibilities, to be open to what is not known, the willingness to discover and to be in the land of not-yet-perfect. The fire is kindled, then it goes out. This is as it should be because the knowledge of the fire's mystery is not complete yet. Part of the excitement is not knowing exactly what's going to happen next. The unknown is a big part of the pull of the Adventurer. Sex may or may not happen, and so many variables put tension in the air.

The scent of orgasm is also in the air. An orgasm would be great, but it is not the central theme either.

Your Fantasies

In the Adventurer, even the mere act of having a fantasy is arousing. The fantasies of the Adventurer are as varied as the unfettered creative erotic mind. Fantasies are fuel for new experiments to discover your erotic self. Fantasies hold a place between reality and magic, where you can mix ingredients into endless combinations and sort out what is appropriate to play out and what is not.

It is said that fantasies, once lived out, are transformed into wonderful daydreams you can refer back to forever. Try some and see for yourself!

Orgasms

No matter how many times you've had sex, you probably still think orgasms are special. We agree. So, we'll give extra attention here to orgasms, inviting Michelle and Michael to lead off, continuing their story of fine tuning their sexual gas pedals and brakes.

Stroking Michael in those forbidden new places felt scary and dangerous. What if he froze up? Or got mad? I was monitoring Michael's every quiver and gasp. I'd do just enough invasion of this new private territory, but not too much, either. Not too much and not too little. Just right! Paying such close attention to him was super erotic.

In the back of my mind, I was thinking about the idea of "boundaries" and the protected "spaces" which are so important for sexual play. I was probing the "edge" of our relationship's sexual boundaries at the same time—testing what was really okay and what was over the top. When I slipped Michael inside me, it felt much bigger than regular intercourse. Like my vagina was a really big space—really huge, beautiful, and grand.

We took our time, and luxuriated in each other and ourselves. We didn't need to push for the mega "yes" of genital orgasm. But we didn't ignore it either. We were able to linger right at the edge of the cliff. Not dive off into the orgasmic sea, and not back off too far either. We stayed there long enough to look directly into each other's eyes for what seemed like forever, and even whisper a few words of love in between breaths. When we finally slid over into final bliss, it was more like melting than fireworks.

— Michelle

Many couples struggle over the timing of their orgasms. Often one person has a faster tempo than the other. Too often this pattern is given the oversimplified and misleading name of "premature" orgasm or ejaculation.

The Adventurer is a place to mutually explore the *edge of orgasm* so you and your partner get more familiar with this special yes/no "territory." Go slowly. This the place to fine tune your radar to map out where you can locate the frontier of runaway bliss. Remember, the Adventurer is not necessarily about orgasms. You don't need to have an orgasm or even ejaculate (although it's OK too). More important is to learn when you and your partner are each near orgasm. That's your yes/no orgasm boundary. Know it well.

Extra credit: Since practice makes perfect (especially true with sex), you and your partner may also want to practice fine tuning your sense of *nearness to orgasm* on your own. Some people call this masturbation. We like to use the clearer term "self-pleasuring." In any case, a great exercise is to go right up to the edge of that no-turning-back point but not over. Then relax and back off. Then go to the edge again. Then back off. Do it three or more times, then go all the way. This is especially helpful for men. You may want to practice alone or with your partner watching. Either way is fine.

THE JOURNEY OF THE SEXUAL ARCHETYPES: THE GATEWAY TO SEXUALITY

The Adventurer is the gateway into self-knowledge. What do you like? What turns you on? What is yours and what belongs to society? Adventurers are on a mission of self-discovery: You push the envelope in order to find out about yourself, your sexual tastes, likes, and dislikes—and those of your partner.

The refrain of the Adventurer archetype is "I dare you!" This is where you probe your limits, and your partner's limits. It is said that the life struggle is to discover what we each like and what we don't like. As ordinary as this sounds, it takes a lifetime of experimenting to figure this out. It isn't easy. There's much more depth in what you like than it may appear at first (just as there's much more depth to pleasure than it appears at first).

What you like and don't like are the ABC's of your aesthetics. Your yes's and no's spell out what you find beautiful, and ultimately, what turns you on. The Adventurer is where you learn your own alphabet of desires. Without this, you might not be able to articulate your vision for ecstatic times together with your partner—if not in words, at least in so-called body language.

But these newfound aesthetics don't come without a price. You must take leave of Michael's beloved innocent Island of Yes and confront the experiences and sensations that are not entirely to your liking. Here in the Adventurer is where you can learn to winnow the golden wheat of your sex life from the not-for-you chaff. And you will be amply rewarded. You will be the stronger for it. Plus, you will be better prepared for the intensity of the Sensualist (in the next chapter) as well.

This winnowing and sorting also applies to your relationship. Maybe you like sex with the lights on, but your partner prefers inky darkness. The Adventurer can be a place to mature your relationship, moving from simple assumptions of your "yes" and your way, to intimate eye-to-eye negotiations of other creative possibilities you've never thought of before.

It is often surprising how little people know of their partners' detailed tastes. It may be the same with you. And conversations alone may not be enough to discover the subtleties of your partner's appetites. A "test drive" may be in order here, and the Adventurer may be the perfect place to take a spin.

You might say, "OK, I have an idea: Let's try making love with just those two ceremonial candles lit on the bedside table. We can see how that goes." And later... "Now that I've tried it, I realize that I actually like it better than the old harsh electric night light. I can still enjoy the intense expressions on your face, only now in a rosier softer glow. And there are still plenty of shadows to enhance the mystery of the moment that you so love to savor."

In the Adventurer, you will leave Michael's Island of Yes in another way as well. Here you may have your first encounter, and even collide, with the larger society and its norms. Inevitably, some of what enraptures you will be at odds with the rules and laws of the larger tribe. It may be fantasies or real desires.

Perhaps you yearn to show your love and affection for your partner in public, but courtesy inhibits you. Or, you yearn to make love naked on a tropical beach with the waves caressing your toes. Do you dare? Maybe. Or maybe not. In either case, reconciling your deepest desires with society, and sharing this with your partner is part of the province of the Adventurer archetype.

Of course, the power of the Adventurer archetype is not lost on Madison Avenue. In our culture, this archetype flourishes. It is the one the marketers play on to sell lots of things. Try this new gadget. Get more for your money. Run in slow motion on faraway tropical beaches. Don't think. Keep consuming, always looking for new sensations. Advertisements often tap into our desires for the never-done-before, exploiting an existential hunger for novelty that forever dwells in all of our souls.

On a more positive note, the Adventurer visits all of us frequently in entertainment and myth. Common images are Sally Bowles in *Cabaret,* and the rowdy, sometimes defiant modern rapper teenager. Madonna often plays the Adventurer archetype as the provocative edge-pusher. And of course, there are loads of adventure movies, spy thrillers, and films that keep us nail biting, on the edge of our seats. You know this archetype well in the outer world. Your invitation in this chapter is to experience the Adventurer in the inner sanctum of your bedroom.

How to Get Started

We hope you are snuggled in bed reading this together, and eager to try the Adventurer out for yourselves. So far, hopefully you've got a sense of the Adventurer. But perhaps you don't know how to kick off the fun.

Last chapter we talked about what we called the Theater of the Bedroom. Don't worry about where you are, but do use your imagination to get in the mood. Think grand; think bigger than life. This will help you vault over the hurdle of day-to-day life to the expansiveness of the Adventurer archetype.

Costumes and Props

Hopefully in the last chapter, if you weren't already hooked on dressing up, you discovered the power and hypnotic spell of costumes to set just the right mood. Well, the Adventurer calls you to go back into your closet to find its appropriate wardrobe.

Let's see how Michael and Michelle got started creating the ambience for their encounter with the Adventurer archetype.

We wind back time to earlier in the afternoon, when they had just arrived home from their visit with Dr. Oona. Michael had always wanted Michelle to be more adventurous in their relationship. And yet he was no doubt still wondering—maybe even worrying a bit by now—what Michelle might have been cooking up back when she had been so strikingly quiet at the end of the session, when Dr. Oona had advised them to dream up some outrageous costumes and head out somewhere to push their buttons. What was Michelle thinking anyway?

When we got home, Michelle was different. That glint in my eyes woke up some wild animal hibernating inside her. I remember noticing her enigmatic smile in Dr. Oona's office, and wondering what she was thinking. Now I was beginning to find out. I thought I was more adventurous than Michelle. Just goes to show how little I knew about her.

When we got home, she flipped on the boom box to the B52s, walked up to me and just stripped me naked then and there. Didn't say a word. I was a little shocked, but I liked it, too. Then she tugged me over to the closet and started changing her clothes. She put on a little skimpy dress with a slit way up the side, sassy neon lipstick, killer high heels, and mussed up her hair for good measure. She motioned to me to slip on a tight pair of jeans, a tough-guy T-shirt, some cowboy boots, and a bad-ass hat. I wasn't sure what she was up to, but I knew it would be good.

— Michael

Here Adventurers translate the "I dare you" mantra into provocative clothing and costumes that push the envelope. The Adventurer archetype is an invitation to push beyond our normal decorum—not way beyond the edge, just enough, just a *little* over the top. You don't push the envelope to break it. Rather we push to *find* the envelope.

It's like being in a dark cave looking for the cave walls. You don't want to crash into the walls and hurt yourself. Rather, you want to *feel* the cave walls. Likewise, you should choose clothes that are as close to your comfort edge as you can get—but not way beyond so you crash into your comfort zone. No need to get the police involved in your fun. But there's no need to be overly timid, either. Remember, you are probing for valuable information: to find *your* limits, your partner's limits, and your joint limits.

Michelle and Michael put on their version of wild clothes. You will have yours. Perhaps you will put on Doc Martens or stilettos and select outrageous tunes for the stereo. Whatever you do, remember that taboos were made for nudging and testing in this archetype. Wild clothes and wild hairstyles are *de rigueur*. Think teenager here. Think rebellious adolescent. Enjoy.

CREATING THE MOOD

♂ *Two can play at this Adventurer archetype. Michelle had thrown down the gauntlet, but I wasn't a slacker. We'd put on these great provocative outfits. Let the night begin! I dared Michelle to walk to the club dressed like that instead of slinking into our car. I wanted to see her walk in public wiggling her cute derrière.*

I was scheming a little adventure of my own. The shortcut to the club went through the city park. When we came to this big empty baseball diamond, in the full glare of lights, I pulled Michelle gently to my side and gave her a big wet French kiss. We'd never made out in public, so this was pushing the edge.

— Michael

Of course, there are lots more ways to break taboos than just a few edgy clothes. Clothes are just the beginning. But don't underestimate clothes either. They are a great way to get you in the mood to try other adventurous activities. Lots to explore.

Okay, now go ahead, think of taboos that make you and your partner squirm a bit. Michael and Michelle had never made out in public before. That challenged their taboos. Such a cute innocent couple they are—or used to be!

(Lest you think kissing has always been an ordinary event [even in private], in 1902 the State of Virginia debated passing an anti-kissing law, a law which would have permitted kissing "only on the certificate of the family physician." Cf. *Journal of the American Medical Association*, December 2002 and 1902.)

Michael and Michelle's edge was pretty close—public "PDAs" were new to them. And of course, many of you are similar to them. However, if that's well inside *your* envelope of ease and comfort, then look elsewhere for your adventure. Be daring for *you*. Possibilities abound! Here are some ideas to kick start your imagination.

Perhaps you are too well mannered to soil yourselves with earthy pornography. Then perhaps this is the time to open that "closed" symbol. Go ahead, buy an X-rated video or a skin mag. Leaf through the pages and let your eyes see what they really see—anew, together. Or go to a sex toy store and load up.

Or maybe this is the time to try that midnight skinny-dipping plunge you've dreamed of but haven't had the courage to do—or even admit to your partner. If that's *no problemo*, then perhaps a daytime trip to a naturist or nudist resort is beckoning you.

Or try a workshop on *Love, Intimacy, and Sexuality* put on by the Human Awareness Institute (www.hai.org). The legendary Stan Dale and his protégés create the most wonderful, heart-filling experiences that challenge even the most cosmopolitan sophisticates in unexpected ways.

If you're feeling even more radical, consider attending a swingers convention. Remember you don't have to participate or jump into the deep end right away. Just keep track of what attracts you and what repels you. But no fair hiding your true reactions and feelings from each other, even if it's slightly embarrassing. "Honey, I know it's totally out of character for me to say this, but, um, er, what would you say about us going to that wild pool party, just this once?"

CLOSED SYMBOLS: THE YES/NO BORDER ZONE

We've talked about how the Adventurer will help you sort out your yes's and no's, as you confront situations on the edge of your comfort zone. Often these challenges at the frontiers of your comfort zones are rooted in your value systems. Here you may be bumping up against your own symbols. These are "things" which are bigger than life, things that carry meaning for you way beyond their physical being.

For example, for some people, a woman wearing just a T-shirt is making the provocative "act" of going bra-less. Furthermore, it's a flagrant *symbolic* message of promiscuity, feminism, etc. For these people, going bra-less is a *closed symbol*. For other people, going happily "bra-free" can be an *open symbol*. In the Adventurer archetype, we suggest you pay special attention to those yes's and no's which have extra charge—the ones that push your buttons.

As Michelle and Michael discover, you can harness the energy of these symbols in your sexual play—it's rocket fuel for the bedroom. But be careful not to get burned!

We were in the middle of the park. Michelle seemed up for a good public smooch and sidled right up to me. I was getting hot. To raise the stakes and crank up the heat a bit more, I slipped my hand under her dress.

This time I could feel her drawing toward me, but at the same time I could tell we'd crossed the Rubicon. By the way her body ever so slightly froze up, I knew we'd crossed the frontier into "no" country. But she was still wavering. Maybe it was really the border zone. I could feel the heat of her body molded against mine.

A couple walked by under a streetlight, and now it was my turn to feel a tad uncomfortable. We weren't at the club yet, but we were already dancing. Dancing on the edge of what we knew about each other—and ourselves!

— Michael

Even if you're strongly pulled to enjoy some sweet pleasure, another part of yourself can shut you down and freeze you up in a flash. Sometimes it's that powerful feeling of "that's just not me" or "I just wouldn't do that!" The "that" is often the fingerprints of a closed symbol. A small event can get projected on the big screen of your larger values, often those which shape your very identity and self-concept.

All of us have some closed symbols. These are big swathes of your psyche which are metaphorically "closed for business." Maybe they help define your identity. They are the "that's not me" alien cast-out furniture of your psyches. Most of your closed symbols can happily remain shut, thank you very much. However, a few of them, if opened, can bring you closer to yourself and your loved ones. But which ones? This is the task of the Adventurer to find out.

Fortunately, it's not a hopeless needle-in-a-haystack search for just the right closed symbols for you to open up. Your intuitional radar is often better than you think. And your lover is usually even better than you are at prying open buried symbolic treasure. Opening closed symbols can be life-changing and freeing. And a great aphrodisiac!

Whatever you do in this archetype, make sure it's fun, heartfelt, and lighthearted. This is not heavy lifting. Leave your "no pain, no gain" T-shirt at the gym. Here in sex-land, it's "no play, no roll in the hay." Speaking of sex, Michael and Michelle taught us about closed symbols in their bedroom earlier in this chapter.

I loved the daredevil feeling of the Adventurer archetype. I felt invincible. I could walk up to Michael, strip him naked in the living room, and just do it without the slightest shred of shame or embarrassment. Damn the torpedoes, full speed ahead.

I felt a real zing in my body as I sauntered across that park half-naked myself, in that slit-up-the-side skimpy dress. Try to stop me, I whispered to myself.

I was as sensitive as ever, maybe more so. When we were kissing in the park, and people were walking right by, I felt the subtle nuances and emotional crosscurrents of my juices starting to boil up, and at the same time, I felt a little uncomfortable about what these strangers might be thinking to themselves.

— Michelle

On the surface, the emotions of the Adventurer archetype are bold and defiant. Risk-taking seems to carry the day. Indeed, this brazen attitude is important to bring the archetype to life at first.

But what's underneath is the true emotional soul of the Adventurer. Michelle's and Michael's willingness to take risks catapults them into a treasure trove of more complex emotions. These are the emotions to pay closest attention to.

As Michael and Michelle waver over how intimate to get in a public park, they are poised on the frontier of their yes's and no's. At first, it might seem odd that you can learn anything from these ambiguous, even confusing experiences. But this is where the gold is. This is where you can discover the true edges of your comfort zone. How do you find your limits?

Michael and Michelle find the edge of their mutual "envelope" by staying with and honoring the crosscurrents of their most subtle emotions. The key is to hold both the *pull* and the *push*—the "yes, more, oh, please" and the "that's enough for now"—at the very *same* instant.

Michelle and Michael have the courage neither to flee from the moment, nor to dive all the way in. They don't freak out. Nor do they just trample their hesitancies and plunge into full-on taboo smashing—single-mindedly damning the torpedoes, full steam ahead.

The emotional gold is in these spaces in between. This is the treasure of what you *truly* like and don't like, not something you've imagined or feared from a safe, remote distance. It's the golden treasure of *truth*—your own co-created truth.

Your Container and Comfort Zone

I didn't understand what a container was until this Adventurer archetype. Then we started "test driving" things like tongue kissing or feeling each other up in public. I really didn't know how Michael would react, or even how I would react.

But what I really didn't expect is every time Michael and I would try something new, it would feel like we were bumping into the edge of Dr. Oona's "container." As if we were in a dark cave, reaching out with our hands to bump into the walls, slowly tracing the cave walls. Here we were discovering the "walls" of our container, the limits of what we liked and didn't like, the limits of how daring we were willing to be.

— Michelle

You will find out who you really are—you and your partner—at the *frontier* of your yes's and no's, at the *boundary* of what heats you up and what cools you off. It's the place where you don't know ahead of time how your partner will react. "Will he or she like it or not? Hmmm, I'm not really sure."

This is the *container*. These are the outer limits of our relationship. Inside this space is where you can play and grow together. The bigger the container or comfort zone, the more of you are welcome to show up to each other. The subjective feeling of ecstasy is closely connected to the size of your containers. The larger the container, the more ecstatic your time is together. Hence, you want your container to be as big as you can make it, while still being happily safe and as comfortable as soft down pillows.

In the process of clarifying your tastes, you will discover your own unique *container*, your own envelope. This is precious information. You will need this in future archetypes. As in fairytales, just in case you might ever encounter a dragon on your journey, better take these tools and goodies with you.

YOUR FREEDOM

When Michelle hit her limits and froze up in the park, I thought we were in for one of those long evenings of accusations and tears. But, miraculously we were able to appreciate the rich banquet of emotions spread out before us. And in the midst of those slow-motion moments, I felt freer than I'd felt in years. I think that's because Michelle's and my "container" was finally starting to get big enough to hold more of our fantasies and desires, more of our emotions and raw feelings.

The hot thing was, we found out that our container was bigger than we'd ever imagined. There were all these things we liked that we hadn't even known about each other, or ourselves. And even if there were a few things which were too over the top for us, like making love in the park, we could still fantasize

86

about them. That was new, too. Either way, our own relationship expanded. I'd been suffocating before and didn't even know it.

— Michael

The Adventurer can help you alchemically transform old heavy lead emotional loops of discomfort and blame into the glittering gold of enchantment and free-flowing emotion. In connecting you with your sense of fun and youth, this archetype can help you face towards the unknown with newfound enthusiasm and freshness.

In these subtle spaces where you courageously explore your likes and dislikes, you can open up a richer, more authentic, and freer intimate life with your partner. You can learn to negotiate your emotional life, to co-create your subjective world, and to tap into deeper-freer-flowing emotions than you might have ever known before.

And then comes the bonus.

The miracle is that our "yes" space is almost always far larger than you might have ever dreamed. People often hold themselves back from exploring this space through purposeless inhibitions. Or, people lose their inhibitions unconsciously through excessive alcohol and drugs but then sadly lose the directions to get back there intentionally another time. Happily, the Adventurer archetype can help all of us trace out the frontier of a very large and orgasmic play space for lovers—and keep returning and enjoying it over and over in new ways.

The Adventurer's teaching is: Don't be afraid to waver. Do not fear ambiguity and conflicting emotions. Enjoy swimming in the crosscurrents of your relationships. For therein you may be renewed and revitalized. The Adventurer may become your relationship's fountain of youth.

The Shadow

I really did love that daredevil feeling and the electricity of wearing my skimpy skirt and exposing so much naked skin in public. I can still feel the buzz from when Michael gave me that long tongue kiss in the park. Oh, how I ached for him to touch me all over, then and there. When his hand reached under my skirt, I wanted to scream and climb on top of him. Even though I felt a couple of chills of discomfort, I really almost did.

I wanted to trample over all my hesitations, and for once in my repressed life, really just go for it, no holds barred. After all, isn't that what the Adventurer is about? And what life is about?

Then a light bulb went off. Oh, that's the Shadow! It's that alien place where I really want to ignore how I really feel, and just go for pure thrills. Except at that moment, it didn't feel alien at all—it felt more like me than ever!

— Michelle

The Shadow of the Adventurer is that people tend to be more interested in challenges and adventures than they are in their partners. To be more interested in the outside than the inner process.

Opening doors is in itself a stimulating and exciting activity. The limitation of the Adventurer is to keep opening more and more doors, experimenting more and more, never choosing a door and going through it. The Shadow of the Adventurer is loss of focus and depth, the so-called Don Juan syndrome where the conquest is more important than the experience. They tend to be more interested in challenges and adventures than they are in being with their partner; the risk is the loss of the heart. Be careful not to neglect your lover when you're exploring this archetype.

LESSONS

Michael and I had hit walls before—places where he would push my comfort zone and I would get really scared. Of course, I would never admit I was afraid. No, that would be too honest—or maybe too intimate. I'm embarrassed to say it, but I would totally blame everything on Michael, and if I were angry, I'd blame it on all males too. "All they want is sex."

But in the park, when Michael started deliciously groping me, I got it. I was uncomfortable, but I also loved it! Something clicked inside me when I realized that I have both push and pull, both gas pedal and brake, both yes and no, inside me. And Michael does too. Before, I was the frightened "no" and Michael the big bad "yes." I made Michael "carry" the yes burden for both of us. Not very fair.

I finally started to share the gas pedal and the brake with Michael—share the driving. We didn't need to go to the club anymore. We'd already had our big adventure for the evening—at least for outings. Time to go "in" now. We shot each other a naughty glance and headed back home.

— Michelle

This archetype sits at the first gateway of initiation where you define yourself and your sexuality in relation to the outside world. The self-knowledge gained here prepares you for the Sensualist.

YOUR TURN

There are lots of ways to enjoy the Adventurer. In addition to the ideas from Michelle and Michael, here are a few more ideas to act out together:

- A pick-up scene
- Go to a sex supply or sex toy store on a date
- Try making out in public
- Go out on the town with no underwear
- Dress like you're a teenager
- Have sex in a way you've never ever done it before
- Have some steamy phone sex
- Try this exercise: How long can you kiss?
- How long can you masturbate without coming?
- Masturbate in different ways, different hands, toys, etc.
- Play strip poker

Onward

In the middle of the night, I woke up briefly, my mind running a slide show of this blow-away evening—that daring walk in the park, exploring Michael's hidden treasures, our eyes meeting in unison just before I came a last time.

Michael and I were on a new path now. We were going somewhere completely new. Like in those fairy tales where you set out into the dark woods, headed for distant castles perched high atop craggy mountaintops. But the big feeling I was having was that we were ready to go on this expedition now. We're prepared. When we head off into the wilderness, we only have us and a few tools, like a Swiss Army Knife and a hotel sewing kit. In our case, we've got to knowing what we like and knowing what we don't like. But we'll pick up more tools along the way.

I dozed off again, dreaming of long spiral staircases leading up towering mountain peaks. Michael was with me.

— Michelle

The Adventurer is eager and ready to set out from the castle on the journey itself. It is the time to acquire the tools that will be necessary to encounter the Shadow and visit the dragon of your sexuality. The dragon may be personal conflict, rape, abuse, repression, shame, betrayal. And yet like the fool, we are the Adventurer now, taking on this archetype's swashbuckling mantle. This emboldens us into that slightly foolhardy, bravado feeling of "let's try anything." Let's experiment with a zucchini or even a presidential cigar. I dare you. Sure, why not?

You, as the heroines and heroes, are getting closer to the dwelling of the dragon. Can you feel the singe of the dragon's tongue of flames, at this (almost) safe distance? The journey is exciting. Are you up for the challenge? Are you ready, prepared to stretch your edges a bit? Do you bring with you the confidence of sure reward like any good Knight of the Round Table? Will you awake to possibilities and be ready to dive as the plot thickens?

The adventure begins. The first trials on the journey are met with a combination of excitement and fear. The character of the Adventurer is one of testing, trying out, opening door number three. The focus is on arousal and excitement, focusing on what you like and don't like, what makes you hot and what chills you cold. The psychic task is to deepen knowledge of your sexual self and its potential. It might be discovering a new orifice, finding a new level of subtlety, or a different sexual orientation. Whatever the specific case, the Adventurer tests preferences and limits.

Our Adventurer will also have its first encounter with the Shadow. Our private desires and the public societal mores are in conflict. This me-them mismatch is the first Zen-like koan of your initiation, an initiation that leads to the Sensualist.

CHAPTER FOUR

The Bonfire of Passion

THE SENSUALIST

"Aphrodite's terrain is the evocation of desire,
the provocation of attraction, the invocation to pleasure"
— James Hillman

When we had our next appointment with Dr. Oona, we couldn't stop bubbling about how much bigger our relationship felt now.

Dr. Oona said this was a perfect segue into the Sensualist archetype. The Sensualist archetype is about diving all the way into sex and surrendering fully to our bodies, our senses, and pleasure. No holding back. This scared us a little.

She promised that diving into our senses for this archetype wouldn't contaminate our ability to love each other or anything. She said to go for it, and ironically, we'd discover more spiritual depth than ever before.

I looked over at Michelle to see what she was thinking, but all I saw were her bare shoulders and her hands caressing her naked thighs below her short low-cut dress. Okay, I said, let's give this Sensualist archetype a try.

— Michael

YOUR TURN

If you have struggled with a split allegiance between heavenly love and earthly sex, please put those ruminations aside for long enough to give the Sensualist a chance—a chance to seduce every cell of your body. Trust us that you will not lose any of your higher values here. On the contrary, your most cherished values can deepen and be strengthened here. That said...

Do you revel in the sheer bodily pleasure of sex? Do you get so hungry for raw, hot sex that nothing else matters? Do you crave to voraciously suck up every drop of your partner's juices, smell every crevice, taste every delight? And blow out in a giant fireworks of an orgasm?

If these are your call letters, then the Sensualist may be your "home" sexual archetype. Even if you only *sometimes* feel this way, the Sensualist may still be your home. Try following its beckoning more. If this earthy sexuality is new territory for you, you and your partner are in for a Thanksgiving-dinner treat. Don't miss this one. You'll never know till you try it!

Let's see what's in store for you with the high-voltage, sexual electricity of the Sensualist:

- That feeling of raw, can't-get-enough, hot physicality
- The power to skillfully seduce
- Feeling of oozing sexuality, volcanic lava overflowing
- An unmistakable invitation to desire and be desired
- Sizzling, broilingly hot, steamy, skin-on-skin, get-inside-me-now fireball
- The irresistible pull to dive deep inside your partner's body and being
- A clear "Yes, sex is what I want right now;" no apologies, no holding back

- Devotion and surrender to unmitigated, unstoppable passion
- A longing to be satiated, feeling that you just can't get enough, a bottomless appetite
- Bathing in fluids, juices, sweat, blood, wetness
- Inhaling scents, smells, aromas
- Diving into spinning whirlpools of sublime pleasure
- Having many orgasms, the more the better
- Unabashed pride in liking sex
- Okay, I'm not afraid to say it boldly: "Yes, I want to fuck right now!"

When you're "inside" the Sensualist archetype, you crave:

- Sex: basic, primal, unedited, unexpurgated, genital sex—the "real thing"
- Intense connection with your lover, total presence, total attention, depth
- Feeling of mind-altering, mind-losing, mind-bending intoxication
- To be swept away, transported by magic carpet to another world, another universe
- Raw sensation, direct feed from our nerve endings, unfiltered feeling
- Arousal, to be turned on, mega-intensity
- To pig out, get it all, engorge, feed at the trough, inhale each other
- To be satiated, filled, completed, quenched
- Skin, fluids, tastes, smells, sensations
- To get fucked, raw desire

For those of you in long-term relationships, it can be challenging to get back to the primal basics of the Sensualist. But the rewards are well worth it. Although it may offend mainstream American morality, it can sometimes be easier to find the Sensualist on a first date! But that's why we began this book with the Innocent and the Adventurer. Hopefully, those of you in long-term relationships have been able to rekindle that first-date feeling through those archetypes. Don't forget those valuable lessons for this trip to the King's Table!

SEX AT THE "ROYAL FEAST"

Here's the next word-photo from our album, nicknamed the "Royal Feast." Imagine…

Now that you've tasted from the Adventurer's Reefs of Danger, you have learned your first lessons and are joyously greeted by a royal welcome to a more sparkling than ever Island of Yes. You feel different now. You have grown up. You have endured the perilous tests of the Adventurer's yes's and no's, and now know well what you like and what you don't like, what makes you hot and what cools you off. You are ready to meet any challenge now. Your reward is nothing less than a seat at the King's and Queen's table of their Royal Feast, in your honor.

You are invited—nay, required—to chow down on the finest cuisine, the smoothest wines, the most mouth-watering fruits, and most delectable candies. You are famished from your trials and adventures getting here. You don't hold back. You and your sweetie dive into this Dionysian feast as if there were no tomorrow—and no one caring about your animal-like table manners.

Sex in the Sensualist

Let's rejoin Michelle and Michael now at their Royal Feast in their hideaway hotel room. As we'll learn about later, their pathway to the Sensualist was to push their limits quite a bit, and spend the day at a local clothing-optional resort, merrily skinny-dipping and enjoying their bodies *au naturel*. It's evening now. Michelle and Michael are basking in the glow of their beautiful, sensuous day together. They have royally invited the Sensualist into their regal bedroom chambers.

I'm not sure if it was spending the day in the altogether— all of me kissed all over by the sun and the water for long luxurious hours—or if it was the Innocent archetype we'd explored before. It was probably both. But even though my genitals were about to catch on fire, it was really strange, they weren't the whole picture either. My whole body was.

Actually it was more like my whole body—every inch of my skin— had become my sex organs. I felt like one giant red-hot clit. All that flooding sexual energy, which usually centers in the area around my vagina, was pulsing through my entire rippling, undulating, buzzing body. Like someone had put in a new electric power grid. My whole being was lit up.

The energy wasn't stuck in one place like it used to be, it was flowing freely, gushing out of my loins. In fact, nothing was stuck. All of me was in motion, like those underwater plants you see scuba diving. All of me in motion. Squirming, writhing, wanting, craving.

I wanted Michael inside all of me. And that's exactly what it felt like when he did enter. We became the waves of the ocean. Very physical, but not hard and solid. We were pure water, pure being, pure sexual energy. Michael was also pure cowboy, riding me hard. And I was pure whore. Give it to me with all your raw, untamed power! In a fleeting wisp of consciousness, before he erupted deep inside me, I got it that we were—yes, I want to use this word—we were fucking and we were making love at the same time.

— Michelle

Michelle will tell us more of her and Michael's grand orgasmic finale in a short while. But first, we want to take time out to say a few words about how you can enjoy sex and the Sensualist. Here are a few reminders for when you slide between the sheets. Actually, you'll probably be so hot you'll toss the sheets and blankets on the floor, and just dive directly into each other.

Here are a few notes for your pillow-side crib sheet. Sensualist sex is:

- Passionate, delicious, embodied, immediate, sensuous
- Genitally focused—and also engaging the whole body and mind
- Hot, steamy, sizzling, fiery, voracious, powerful
- Unstoppable, uninhibited, uncensored, unexpurgated
- Energetic, athletic, erotic, excited, aroused
- Shameless, fun-loving, happy, wild-eyed, celebratory
- Complete in its own right, nothing missing
- Straight from the Garden of Eden: where we eat the apple with no remorse

Your best teacher is your body. Listen to it. You will do great. But just in case, here are a few pre-flight tips for an even smoother trip:

- *Don't* talk about remodeling the kitchen.
- *Don't* worry about becoming a pleasure slut, you are one.
- *Don't* be ashamed, don't let your mom's voice tell you to cool it.
- *Don't* necessarily take a shower to be squeaky clean ahead of time.
- *Don't* get up to wash things off, stay "swimming" in the ocean.
- *Don't* be in a hurry, don't look at the clock, don't think about where it's going.
- *Don't* withdraw, don't break the mood, don't straighten up the sheets.
- *Don't* joke around, don't go for easy quick releases.
- *Don't* hide your body, don't hide your pleasure.

- *Do* make sounds, moan and groan, grunt, scream.
- *Do* appreciate his hard-on and her juices.
- *Do* ask for what you want, be explicit.
- *Do* say yes, or I'd prefer this, just grunt out what you desire.
- *Do* encourage your partner to go for it.
- *Do* lust after each other; be animals, animals are beautiful.
- *Do* leave your relationship issues at the door; practice safe sex.
- *Do* be confident in your sexuality, you know what feels good.
- *Do* whisper in your lover's ear that you love her or him.
- *Do* go all the way, go for the top of the mountain.
- *Do* be an exhibitionist with your sexuality, and a voyeur.

- *Do* see yourself as a beautiful sex god or goddess—
  you are.
- *Do* suck and kiss and touch everywhere.
- *Do* enjoy fluids, juices, smells, scents.
- *Do* have sex during menstruation—even paint your body
  in her blood.
- *Do* let yourself get carried away.
- *Do* love, enjoy, and adore your partner.

This is what many people think that sex is—of course, in a far more subdued form. All of what sex is. The whole enchilada. That's it. In fact, in its sanitized, toned-down, "acceptable" packaging, the Sensualist is the "home" archetype of our culture. After all, sex is basically physical, right? It's about putting "tab A" into "tab B" like the directions on assembling a cardboard box, right? And getting off.

So, the Sensualist is probably somewhat familiar to you. But perhaps the raw intensity and fullness of the Sensualist are new to you. This intensity is the key to this archetype: Going all the way with a no-holds-barred commitment to pleasure and juice.

Our culture is (destructively) split in a kind of "to be or not to be" of the body, that is: To have a body or not to have a body. More precisely the conundrum is: To go for *total* pleasure or not. This is sometimes called the Madonna/whore dilemma. Should you go for broke with earthly pleasures, or hold back so as not to tarnish the poetic, heavenly beauty of love with unsightly, carnal, barnyard crudity? Not an easy choice, at least put that way.

Fortunately the Sensualist does not make you choose. You can have both. We'll explain more about that later. In the meantime, leave all your concerns at the bedroom door, and dive into each other.

Your Arousal

Your arousal is generated directly by your genitals, and is swift and sure. The mantra of the Sensualist is "I am horny" and "I am hot." There is a simplicity to arousal in this archetype.

Once your yes's and no's are clarified in your life, you can more easily express what you desire and go for what you truly want. There is no beating around the bush, no subtle courtship and seduction, no lengthy romantic candlelight dinners, no drawn-out foreplay in this direct in-your-face archetype. Time to "get on down" and have some good old sex!

Your Relationship with Your Body

You've probably already noticed that the Sensualist is profoundly about your body. No question about it. Your body leads here. Your body does the "thinking" here. But this is not to say that there is no subtlety. Far from it.

It can be surprisingly hard to "let go" and really listen to the sirens of your physicality. Don't worry, it takes practice to do simple things like just being purely physical. It's not that easy. So go ahead and practice. And don't be ashamed if you're slow at it. Who could wish for a better practice regimen! In spite of how often people get accused of acting like "animals," and even though the Sensualist has an animal-like sexuality, it's just not that easy for humans to act like "animals." And remember, animals are beautiful, too.

The flip side of the coin is, be careful not to pig out so much you forget your partner is in the room. Ultimately the Sensualist —as with all the sexual archetypes—is about connection with your partner. Stay in your body. Don't space out. As the gurus like to say, "Be here now." In all ways.

Your Emotions

Lest you think the Sensualist is purely unemotionally physical, think again. The Sensualist celebrates gut-wrenching passion. The inner emotional feeling is stark and powerful, "I want you, I want you, I can't get enough of you."

The Sensualist is more importantly about trust, grand trust in the abiding *goodness* of Eros and desire. Along with this trust, here you give each other mutual permission to go deeper in your relationship, deeper than perhaps you ever thought you could together. In effect, the Sensualist teaches you that pleasure is far deeper than you might ever have imagined. There is much emotional depth here. Don't miss it!

Your Erotic Fire

As the title of this chapter indicates, your erotic fire burns at bonfire intensity in the Sensualist. In the Innocent, you learned to play with matches. Then in the Adventurer, you learned to ignite the fire. Now it's time to "Burn, baby, burn!"

The challenge in the Sensualist is to keep focused so the conflagration can keep burning to build up a very high level of charge, so as to have a blow-out level of orgasmic discharge. This brings up the ever-favorite topic of orgasms.

Your Orgasms

As always, but especially with the Sensualist, orgasms deserve special attention. So, let's go back to Michelle and Michael to see what they have to say here.

When you ask me about my orgasms, I'm not sure what to say. Or rather where to start. Back in that naturist resort's parking lot when I mustered my courage and stripped completely—and I felt the warmth of the sun caress me from my spinning brain down to my toes, I'm sure I came right then. Swimming naked in that emerald lagoon was like one continuous orgasm. Maybe the whole afternoon was one long languid orgasm. I'm not sure what that word means anymore.

Later when Michael slammed into my craving vagina, my G-spot, deep inside, started throbbing in white-light pleasure. Then the feeling spread to my clit and then to my whole body. After that, orgasms would come in waves, rolling through my whole insides. Things would be calmer for a few seconds. And then a mighty orgasmic wave would roll through me like I was the ocean itself.

The amazing thing was that these orgasms were completely full-body. My genitals might have been pumping out megawatts of energy, but it felt like the actual orgasms were coursing through my entire flailing nervous system.

We shook Mt. Olympus itself. For an archetype that is about the physical body, I think we sent some mega-strong signals to the gods they won't forget for a while.

— Michelle

The most common question we get on Sensualist orgasms is, "Are they genital or full-bodied? Which is it?" The enigmatic and paradoxical answer is a "yes" on both scores. Michelle put her finger on it, so to speak, when she said her whole body felt like her sex organs. She said she felt like one "giant red-hot clit."

The nuclear fires of the Sensualist are your genitals. This is where the energy revs up. This is the source of the fiery flames which go on to torch the rest of your body—your whole body. And that's the key: your whole body. Many people confine their sexuality just to their genitals. It gets bottled up there, and wastes its enormous power, like an electric generating station with no power lines to distribute the power to the cities. When you hook up those power lines to the rest of your body, your whole being lights up. That's what we're trying to encourage you to do here.

It can take a lot of sexual charge to energize your whole body. But what an orgasm you can have when you discharge all that energy in one blow-out wham! Or a bunch of whams. You had probably better warn your neighbors in advance that you're playing with nuclear energy.

Here's a glance at Sensualist orgasms. They:

- Boil up from the intense heat of the genitals, rooted in the genitals
- Often come in oceanic waves, washing over us, flooding us
- Are cathartic, leaving us feeling transformed
- Are often multiple orgasms; the more the better
- Are explosive, the Big "O" wakes the neighbors
- Are as wet and juicy as possible; as hard as possible
- Are athletic, hard-driving, energetic, hard work
- Are noisy, expansive, animalistic, instinctual, primal
- Are captivating, center of the world

THE JOURNEY OF THE SEXUAL ARCHETYPES: CELEBRATING SEXUALITY

The Sensualist could have been called the hedonist, the luscious, or more provocatively and less politely, the pleasure slut. It's the sexual archetype dedicated to the pure pursuit of physical pleasure.

In the Sensualist you build a bonfire of passion, a conflagration of rapture. You unleash your desires as if there's no tomorrow. "I want you! Now! No time to undress politely.

Tear off your clothes!" It seems like a simple enough archetype. It's just about the physical body and bodily sensation. It's distilled, raw, in-your-face gluttony. It can't be that hard or complicated. Right?

At first blush, the Sensualist would seem to be the easiest archetype in our culture, too. After all, we live in a physical culture. We glorify athletes and sports heroes. Our movie stars exemplify physical beauty.

Obediently, our sex education courses in high schools follow the "medical model" and typically focus on the narrowly clinical side of human sexuality, namely the physical act of human reproduction. How to do it: Insert the male pipe into the female fitting, like some household plumbing project. The courses dwell on a litany of what can go wrong: very bad things like gonorrhea, herpes, HIV, etc. And the overall message is a simplistic moral: Kids, don't try this at home (i.e.: "Just say no").

Despite its apparent straightforward physicality, the Sensualist archetype is a deceptively deep and rich archetype. Its dynamics go to some of the very roots of some of our culture's hardest conundrums. These are the issues which keep many a couple up into the wee hours of the morning, washed in tears of unraveling love lives. And issues that send them to their therapists in an often futile quest to get some shred of insight into these most basic human impulses.

We are drawn to raw physicality like Odysseus was to the Sirens. And yet in the very same breath, we deeply fear losing ourselves to our "animal" nature. We lash ourselves to the mast as Odysseus did, lest we be forever pulled off our raft by the alluring call of raw pleasure.

We are split down the middle between heaven and earth, between spirit and flesh, between responsibility and hedonism, between demur dining and whole-hog gluttony. Even between Hera and Aphrodite. They spent nine years of the Trojan War fighting each other. Perhaps the war continues—in our culture and our psyches even today!

Images of the Sensualist archetype are, of course, all over our movie screens. The cinemagraphic medium bathes us in sensuous eye-candy photography. Moreover, the images of simulated lovemaking so often convey tingling, naked, yearning skin, almost singeing the silver screen with tongues of erotic fire.

The *split* between responsibility and hedonism is also all over the screen. Most notably, sex is typically accompanied by violence, sending the subliminal message that raw pleasure leads to violent distress.

Of course, this *split* between heaven and earth is glaringly mirrored in our everyday language. When nestled in bed with our lovers, enjoying sweet pillow talk, do we speak of "making love" or do we use that crude barnyard word, "fuck"? But is this taboo word so crude after all? Doesn't *fuck,* in fact, convey the raw physicality of sex far better than all those weak, gussied-up, namby-pamby words like *intercourse, doing it, coitus,* etc.? Euphemisms are the fingerprints of splits in our collective psyches. And oh, what a split! It's more like an earthquake fault.

This schizoid split also colors our very self-concepts. As with Michael above, many of us hunger for sex. But don't you dare call us sluts! As a culture, we've even professionalized the anathema of seeking raw pleasure "too much" by often labeling and pathologizing unabashed Sensualists as "sex addicts."

In our culture, sex and spirit are often seen as polar opposites. We are often told that earthy sex and heavenly soaring with the deities are not on the same planet. They are totally different parts of the human experience. And yet, we yearn to combine and integrate them.

Our Judeo-Christian institutions are often blamed for promoting this sex/spirit polarity. But many New Age cults promote an even more radical version of this polarity, preaching abstinence as the pathway to enlightenment. On the other hand, a number of ancient and indigenous cultures make no such division at all. In some Native American cosmologies, the East, which is the symbolic domain of the rising sun and new beginnings, is also the domain of what we in the West separately call sex and spirit. These cultures have one integrated concept!

Notably, some modern communities and organizations are heroically putting Humpty Dumpty back together again for us, i.e., integrating sex and spirit. Examples include the American tantric communities as well as organizations like the Human Awareness Institute (hai.org) based in the San Francisco Bay Area. These groups are not only integrating sex and spirit, but love and intimacy as well. More on Tantra, etc. in the upcoming chapter on the Mystic archetype.

Regardless of our best efforts and sky-high therapy bills, most of us continue to be caught in the snare of the "Madonna and the whore" cultural schism. Are you a "good" girl or "nice" girl? The Sensualist archetype is a kind of "gateway" through which we can begin to integrate these often warring, disparate parts of ourselves: the cold and the hot, the morally correct "good" and pleasure-pleasing "nice" aspects of ourselves.

The Sensualist archetype is an invitation to tune into our senses and pig out.

Oddly enough, the Sensualist is also an invitation to deepen our spiritual lives, to drink from the aquifers that quench our human souls, to increase our wonder and majesty of the universe, to revitalize the sparkles in our and our partner's eyes. If we truly accept this unusual invitation, many treasures await us in our sex and spirit lives alike, as well as in the upcoming archetypes.

How to Get Started

If like many couples, you want better, more passionate sex, the Sensualist will be your teacher. That's as it should be. And as we've seen, the Sensualist is a great teacher here. But how do you get started? How do you ignite the bonfire?

We'll let Michelle and Michael do most of the teaching in this section. They took their Theater of the Bedroom outdoors, and show us the great way they primed their bodies and spirits for truly embodied sex later in the day.

Of course, you don't need to go skinny-dipping to call in the Sensualist. There are lots of ways, including dance, athletics, even meditation. But please do consider Michelle and Michael's story seriously. Nudity is one of the best ways of all to celebrate your exquisite body. The mantra of the Sensualist is "use it and flaunt it!"

Remember, don't let fears, peer pressure, and social conventions drive your relationship. It's *your* relationship. It doesn't belong to anyone else. For all the sexual archetypes, *courage* is the most powerful aphrodisiac of all.

Costumes and Props

At first Michael and I were dumbfounded by this Sensualist archetype. It seemed totally easy. It's just getting physical. But how to get started? In the first two archetypes, we dressed up in clothes to get into the mood. Clothes hypnotized us into the mindset of each archetype. But if the Sensualist is just about raw sensation, then what do we wear? Michael laughed, "I guess we're just supposed to go naked. Where are we gonna go to do that?"

I blurted out, "Hmmm, maybe we can!" I loved the look on Michael's face, a cross between "you've got to be kidding" and "you are kidding, aren't you?"

"We can go to a nudist resort. I think there's one I heard about near here." Michael had to reach down and pick up his jaw. I was doing my best to hide my own nervousness.

My unruffled exterior worked a little too well. After a long pause, Michael said, "I guess you're right. A nudist resort has the right dress code for enjoying our senses and all our skin. If we can get over walking around stark naked in front of a bunch of total strangers!"

What started out as a joke was turning into an expedition to the moon—this very afternoon! What had I gotten myself into? But I wasn't about to show I was scared now. And I have to admit, I was a little curious too, even excited. The Sensualist archetype was already taking hold.

— Michelle

You don't have to go to a nudist or naturist resort. But Michelle and Michael are on the right track. Think skin. Think of ways to luxuriate in sensation. It might be a hot tub or a massage. Or it might be skin-tingling skinny-dipping.

SETTING THE STAGE

I can't believe we actually got in our car and drove right into the front gate of this nudist resort. Actually they called it a naturist resort. I guess that's because they think not wearing clothes is natural or something. I saw a towel there that said, "If we were meant to go nude, we'd have been born that way." Very funny. But I guess they have a point.

Anyway, after I finished noticing that the people at the front office didn't even have a stitch of clothes on, I realized how friendly they were, too. Then something funny happened to my brain. I felt odd being fully dressed when everyone else was, well, totally naked.

They suggested we toss our clothes in our car, and then they'd give us a tour. I said "Sure, no problem." I hope they didn't hear my gulp. I went over to the side of the car that was a little more private and slowly unbuttoned my blouse, then eased off my shorts.

As I slipped off my last thread of the normal world, my favorite blue silk undies, all of a sudden, I felt my whole body come alive, all my skin was euphorically singing. I couldn't believe it! It felt totally fantastic to be free, especially on this hot summer day. My skin tingled, like it had been waiting for this for decades! Like it was screaming out, What took you so long? I hardly noticed that Michael was staring at me. He looked so great au naturel.

— Michelle

A big fork in the road in entering the Sensualist is whether to listen to your old preconceived ideas, or listen directly to your body in the moment. Your choice. Michelle could have gotten stuck in secondhand information—old prejudices or what others might think. But instead, she took the courageous fork in the road and listened to her body directly, right then. She got the most "up-to-date" information available—late-breaking news directly from her body's nerve endings. And on this hot summer day, her skin spoke loudly and clearly.

EMOTIONS

Wake me up. I was actually walking totally nude past a swimming pool full of splashing naked people. The mind-blowing thing was that it took me only about two minutes flat to love it.

If the Adventurer is daring, the Sensualist is full-scale Indiana Jones. This naturist park made skimpy dresses seem like Girl Scout uniforms.

But this was light years away from the Adventurer, too. We'd broken through some kind of barrier. All those pushes and pulls, and yes's and no's of the Adventurer were a million miles away.

Before, the skimpier the clothes, the more scandalous we were. Now here, skimpier wasn't the word for it! Yet in this sweet, sun-drenched air, there was not the slightest hint of scandal or provocation. It was just pure ecstatic, sensuous, skin-tingling freedom. When I dove into the pool, I felt like a primordial fish swimming in the tropics. My smooth bare skin glided effortlessly through the blue-green waters.

I imagined I was in a South Seas emerald lagoon making love to the water gods. I got out of the pool and felt the warm sunlight caressing my whole body, sun-kissing all the little beaded-up water droplets on my freshly awakened skin. No need for a towel. I just walked over to Michael and gave him a dripping wet hug.

— Michelle

Michelle made a big emotional breakthrough. They used some of the daring they had cultivated in the Adventurer archetype to get up the courage to go on their expedition. But now, they have broken through their initial hesitation, to a newfound Island of Yes of the clarity of pure unashamed sensation.

Setting the Space

Michelle had scared the willies out of me with her nonchalant talk of test-driving the Sensualist archetype at a nudist resort.

But then, a few short freedom-loving hours later, there we were, joking with a bunch of people in the hot tub, telling them we were never going to wear clothes ever again. They'd have to force us to get dressed. Luckily there were overnight cabins there, so at least we could avoid clothes for a few more blissful hours.

I've never been so continually conscious of my whole body for that many hours straight. But at a deeper level, we were listening to our own inner song, too. We had found a new "space" in our relationship. It held the deeper knowing that we were truly doing what we liked. And what we didn't like was a million miles away. When I gave Michelle a hug, it felt like her body was on fire—all of it. Whew, lucky we were in our own private hideaway now!

— Michael

The Shadow

As with all the sexual archetypes, don't forget to stay keenly conscious of your partner. No amount of passion is license to forget who you are so passionate about!

The minute we were alone together, this erotic firestorm swept through my body like a whirlwind. I was pure bodily desire. Nothing else. I desperately wanted one thing, and one thing only: to be inside Michelle whatever it took. If she'd had any clothes on, I would have ripped them off right then.

The delicious slow sensuousness of the day flipped into pure raw gotta-have-her passion. Michelle was kissing me so deeply, I just about came right then. No apologies for being a guy who just wanted to stick it in.

Those words were just about to tumble out of my mouth, when something shrieked inside me. Even in that mad frenzy of passion, with Michelle squirming and panting and wrapping her legs tightly around me, I remembered the Shadow. I had almost gotten sucked into the old cliché grade-B violent movie image of the disconnected stud. Fuck her and leave her.

I think Michelle was also on the edge of wanting to just devour me, take no prisoners, too. But being really connected, in sync every writhing moment, is so much hotter. Throw some more logs on the bonfire, honey!

— Michael

LESSONS

Michael's a nice guy, but over the years, I've also been trying to change him, mold him to be more like me. I never could have said this before.

I'd been working on Michael to be more starry-eyed when we made love, more candlelight romantic. But that night in the naturist cabin, I realized I'd been missing out on a big part of Michael.

I must have been afraid of that side of him before. But I think my real fear was that I would match him, animal for animal, and totally pig out. And he would see that deep down, I'm an insatiable nympho.

That night I learned a valuable lesson. We went to slut-land like never before. And we discovered this giant paradox. At the same time as Michael, the kick-ass dude, was driving his big 18-wheeler home, he was hot and sweet. Raging bonfires of passion and being perfectly soul-connected!

— Michelle

The big lesson of the Sensualist is combining those two facets of your irrepressible humanity: hot and sweet. You will be so much more powerful if you can marry these two parts of your soul—more powerful in the bedroom, and at your workplace.

The surrender to the bonfire of passion is the koan and initiation of the Sensualist. Indeed, we do surrender, but we never lose track of ourselves in doing so. We stay intact, fully awake. For example, we don't get so carried away that we forget to practice safe sex, and safe consensual emotions. We're still fully there, yet totally at one with our most earthly bodily sensations.

YOUR TURN

Now you get to try out the Sensualist archetype. Here are some ideas to get started:

- Decide to stay in bed for five hours
- See how many orgasms you can have
- Ask for what you want, be explicit and detailed
- Find twenty ways to ask your partner for sex
- Practice seduction
- Perform a strip tease for your partner
- Go to a naturist/nudist resort
- Play like animals, animals having sex together
- Find out which animal you identify with
- Act like you're meeting a stranger; go "all the way" with him or her
- Give each other erotic massages

Onward

We slept entwined, holding each other all night. Michelle's body was wrapped around me like we'd wrestled with wild beasts all day, and had finally returned safely into each others' loving embrace. But what delightful wild beasts they were.

I'm not sure why surrendering to our senses and pleasure takes so much courage and resolve. But the fear was real.

It was very intimidating to face our deepest pleasure-seeking selves. But we did it. We succeeded. We are a step closer to healing the giant schism of Madonna and whore, integrating our love for bottomless pleasure with staying fully connected with our entire bodies, ourselves, and each other—both emotionally and physically.

— Michael

Congratulations, you turned the corner to meet the dragon of the Sensualist in its full fiery intensity. You were ready. When you played with the Adventurer, you learned your limits well, your yes's and your no's. In the Sensualist, you were called to dive totally into the frothing, bubbling lava of carnal love. No holding back. Total surrender to the senses.

You made full frontal contact with Earth and matter. You celebrated your body. Hopefully, you now love your body and all its flowing, wet juices more than ever. You enticed, seduced, and looked straightforward in the eyes of craving *desire*. You met the fire head-on, the furnace breath of the dragon. Hopefully, you feel more awake and empowered now.

We hope you have come away renewed, juicy, sated at the altar of pleasure. Perhaps you feel whole, well, almost whole. If you are like many who visit the Sensualist, a remaining hunger gnaws at you. And propels you down the trail to your next archetypal widening in the trail. The journey continues around the bend to the Seeker.

CHAPTER FIVE

Turning Up the Burners

THE SEEKER

"Seek Him in the Kingdom of Anxiety;
You will come to a great city that has expected your return for years."
— W. H. Auden, *For the Time Being*

We loved all that fun of the Sensualist archetype. We'd never plunged so deeply in the ocean of raw physical sexuality before.

But what's left to do? How could there be more archetypes? We're done, aren't we? But, how could we be?

After our gutsy expedition to that naturist park, we'd made physical love every night with an intensity that would shock the animal kingdom—and probably did shock our neighbors. It was sublime, delicious, like caviar and champagne every night.

And yet something was still missing.

Dr. Oona said the key word was "imagine." We had gotten an A+ for the physical aspect of sex. Great job. Now we were ready to use our minds.

— Michael

It looks like Michelle and Michael are in for some new surprises. Are *you* up for some mystery stories and cliffhangers of your own?

Do you like to play with dramatic tension in the bedroom? Do you like to tantalize and tease your partner, make your partner beg for some erotic treat? Have you ever play-acted power and control fantasies, or even bondage? Do you like whodunnit movies? Do you like suspense? Do you just like a good drama?

For many people, the Seeker is a new twist on their sexuality. Perhaps you will twist and squirm in a new way. The Seeker often cracks opens unexpected sexual territory. So, we suggest you wait to decide if this is your "home" sexual archetype until after you've spent some time getting into it. Let your home archetype be a cliff-hanger for now, too.

Here's an initial glance at the sexual electricity of the Seeker. They:

- Explore the unknown, the void, the mystery of life and sexuality
- Visit the unexplored, hidden corners of their psyches
- Get things going intentionally, deliberately
- Go beyond their normal sexual comfort zone into their freak-out zone
- Are willing to do things that are just plain scary—in the bedroom by choice
- Erotically confront their internal fears
- Risk their absolute bedrock beliefs
- Push their edges, values, habits, sense of normalcy, decorum
- Plunge headlong into their own taboos and old sexual wounds
- Bring their emotional pain with them into their sexual play

- Allow themselves to "crack open," break through to a more intimate plane
- Bring dramatic tension and cliff-hangers into the bedroom
- Act out "scenes" coming from their imagination and fantasies
- Continue on with a sex scene even when they don't know how it will end
- Let Eros carry them when your mind says, "not quite ready yet"
- Trust that the world and their partner are ultimately good and love them
- Go into the underworld, become familiar with their underworld
- Lose control, expose themselves, are deeply vulnerable, emotionally naked
- Enjoy the sexual of heat of the confined oven instead of the unbounded bonfire

When you're inside the Seeker archetype, you desire to be:

- Ravished, "taken," overcome, inhaled, carried away
- Changed, transformed, renewed, never the same again
- Wildly out of control, surrendered, out of your mind
- Totally dependent on your partner and partner's erotic whims
- Opened, vulnerable, taken apart, deconstructed, incoherent
- Unburdened, free of self-judgments, not in charge
- Totally accepted including your contradictions and foibles
- Taken care of, loved, adored, safe, satisfied
- Erotic, charged, intense, consumed by sexual heat

For you, this may sound like a very strange kind of sex. Or not sex at all—more like some weird activity that aliens do on *Star Trek*. But trust us: The Seeker can awaken you in ways you had never dreamt of, and heat your relationship up to a higher temperature than your thermometer has numbers for. The Seeker is very erotic when you "get" it. Read on. And most of all, practice the Seeker in your own bedroom. It's fun. It's exciting. It may singe your bedsheets. The Seeker is very sexy!

SEX IN THE "VOLCANIC CAVES"

Our South Seas nickname for the Seeker takes us deep under the Island of Yes to its steamy hot underworld Volcanic Caves. Imagine…

You're still savoring the enchanted aromas and luscious aftertastes of the Royal Feast of the Sensualist. You gorged until you couldn't put another succulent berry between your lips. And yet unexpectedly, your spirit is still hungry for something more. What is it? Some scratching in the back of your head? Some hunger that food alone cannot sate?

You glance out the window of the royal grass hut and the answer fills your eyes. The volcano at the center of the Island of Yes draws you toward it. You cannot resist. You say a thankful good-bye to the King and Queen and head out into the jungle, drawn by the beauty, mystery, and danger of this rumbling, flaming mountain.

As you approach the volcano, you see an opening, an entrance to a cave, a sure signpost of the way to the underbelly of the Island. You enter without thinking. It is darker than a moonless night. You proceed with your hands outstretched feeling your way, touching the moist, wet rocks of the furrowed cave walls. Your skin is hot, but in a new unfamiliar way, bodily heat combined with a yearning, unsettled mind. You continue on, deeper into the cave's labyrinth.

Sex in the Seeker

Meanwhile, Michelle and Michael are about to explore their own alluring cave in their bedroom paradise…

In past chapters, we have "cut to the chase" and jumped right into Michelle's and Michael's bedroom lovemaking at this point in the chapter. In those chapters, we postponed the "getting started" details about how they got there till later. This chapter on the Seeker is different. Perhaps you can already guess why we're going to start at the beginning of their story of fun with the Seeker?

We join Michelle and Michael relaxing in their living room. Michael begins the story.

Michelle and I decided to take the evening off, hang out at home, and watch this great Sherlock Holmes video. We snuggled up on the sofa, and settled in.

We'd been watching for a hour or so and the suspense really started to build. I didn't want to budge. I was stuck to my chair. But I needed to stretch my legs. I stood up for a sec. Michelle got up to get some popcorn. My eyes stayed glued to the screen. What was going to happen next?

I felt a little chill go up my spine and everything went dark. Before I could think, Michelle whispered in my ear, "Don't move!" She'd slipped a soft velvet blindfold over my eyes. I was stunned. Then the video sound went off. Poof. Total silence and darkness.

I felt Michelle's warm hand on my face, while her other hand started unbuttoning my shirt. All I heard was the ruffling of cloth as she undid my shorts and left me standing there wearing only that tight blackout blindfold.

— Michael

Notice how Michael didn't resist, even though he was quite surprised, not to mention about to miss out on the rest of the movie. Michael stays with the scene, allowing himself to surrender to Michelle's plan, whatever it is. Maybe Michelle doesn't even totally know what she's up to herself. Let's continue.

After blindfolding me, Michelle gently put her arm around my bare butt and walked me across the living room, around a corner, then straight, then left, until I had no idea where I was. The little hairs on my naked thighs tingled as we shuffled along. But that was nothing compared to the electricity sparking inside my head—and throughout the whole rest of my body.

Every memory of ever being vulnerable or exposed was racing though my fluttering insides. I wasn't afraid. I knew I was totally safe in Michelle's caressing hands. But it vividly reminded me of other times when I really had had the willies scared out of me. You know that feeling. You're in the woods in the middle of the night. It's pitch dark and you hear all these creepy sounds. You don't know what's going to jump out from behind a bush.

The cliff-hanger anticipation of every slow-motion second was extremely erotic. And extremely erotic. Every so often, Michelle's fingers would brush against my aching loins, but I never knew when it would be. And every time, a tornado swept through my whole body.

— Michael

Do you see how the erotic energy is flooding out of Michael's mind as much as his body? This weaving together of mind and body is the hallmark of the Seeker. It's hard to do, but can be intensely erotic when you can get it right.

What about Michelle? Did she plot this all out in advance? How much planning should you do to call in the Seeker? Let's see how this scene looked from Michelle's perspective.

I don't know what possessed me, surprising Michael like that right in the middle of that video. I was tired of watching other people's stories and I wanted us to be the stars of our own story for a change.

When I went into the kitchen to grab some popcorn, I saw one of those airline sleeping masks on the counter that Michael had brought home from a recent trip. Something naughty popped into my head. I just went for it. It was so fun to sneak up behind Michael when he was glued to the video and pounce—and pop that mask over his eyes.

I couldn't just stop there. I had to keep the story line going, like some kind of improvisational theater act. Except I'd never seen erotic improv before. I had to be creative. After an initial wave of I-can't-do-that swept over me, I thought, Okay, watch me! In those micro seconds of hesitation, I also realized I was creating one of those "scenes" right then and there.

— Michelle

The Seeker celebrates the unknown. That's the big idea.

Even though Michelle started the scene deliberately (although from an impulse), from then on, she continued creating the scene improvisationally. And of course, Michael had even less of an idea what was about to happen, second by second.

How you can get started with the Seeker is to create drama and suspense. If you leap to the punch line without a proper build up, the punch line falls flat, thud. But by preparing a dash of whodunnit, the main event is hopefully worth waiting for. Now you know why we delayed the sex in this chapter until now...

Sex and the Seeker

Improvising, as Michelle was doing, is only one way the Seeker invites the unknown. The second, more profound way, is the challenge of adding the unknown while in the sexual moment itself. Let's hear from Michael about his experience with a truly mind-shifting encounter with the unknown. As we join Michael, he still doesn't know what Michelle is cooking up for him.

As Michelle was guiding me blindfolded, I was afraid she was going to take me to our bedroom, tie me to the bed-posts, and have one of those bondage scenes like you see in Madonna videos. I even had fantasies of Michelle pulling out one of those soft leather whips and gently flogging me. That was a wild thought! In the last few weeks with those other archetypes, she'd pulled out a bunch of other surprises. So anything was possible. I was totally in the dark about what she was up to—that alone cranked up the erotic charge another notch or two for me.

Michelle stopped me abruptly and tugged me down on my knees. Then she sat down on what seemed like a bed, and pulled my face into her lap. I don't know when she got undressed, but I felt her smooth, bare, warm thighs against my mouth. And a slightly pungent smell. Oh my god, I bet she has her period. Before I could think, she shoved my nose into her fragrant bush.

Call me crazy, but the smallest hint of blood scent right then reminded me of human sacrifices in ancient ceremonies I'd read about.

I'd never tasted Michelle this time of the month. We'd had sex then, but I'd kept my distance from blood. I hadn't really thought about it, but now I was realizing Michelle had noticed that I'd been holding back all these years.

I'd read that some cultures isolated women during their flow. I thought that was cruel—now I was realizing I'd also been doing that. In other cultures, women on their "moon" were in their "power." I bet that's what Michelle was thinking tonight.

I put aside any social conditioning and phobias holding me back, and plunged my tongue courageously into her delicious wet folds. I can't imagine what my face looked like. It didn't matter. All at once I surrendered to Michelle as a representation of some deeper femininity of the human race. And she surrendered to my pure, unrestrained passion. When she was moaning and writhing almost over the top, I moved onto the bed and slid my own sex deeply inside her wetness, with my blindfold still keeping me in perfect darkness.

It was as if some deeper invisible tension in our souls had been relieved. Some drama for mutual acceptance had been miraculously resolved between us. An unspoken, even unconscious fear had been brought up from the underworld, and transformed into the pure light of ecstatic lovemaking. We were making love in a new way. More free. More connected. More present.

— Michael

Here, Michael confronts his fear and distaste for menstrual blood. This is truly scary for him, and demands *courage in the midst of sex*—not just beforehand as in the previous archetypes. Mixing fear, especially transformational fear, with sex can be intensely hot—like a white-hot furnace melting the steel girders of your mind.

When you are choreographing your own erotic scenes, if you want to tap into the hottest, most erotic volcanic lava, remember to stay connected to your deep underlying psychic issues.

Your own fears may be very different from Michael's. Blood may not be your issue. It might be old hat, or not important, or too challenging to "go there" for now. In any case, find your own fear "edge" and mine out that mother lode for your own gold.

Here are some examples of other challenges which might be issues in your relationship:

- Not being good enough, skilled enough, not being able to pleasure well enough
- Feeling just plain klutzy
- Not being able to stay hard or have an orgasm
- Shame about your body or your body image
- Female ejaculation, getting the bed drenched
- Being a slut, or being an unromantic "businessman"

Here are some additional tips:

- *Don't* break any dramatic tension that is building, keep the scene going.
- *Don't* resist, complain, or whine.
- *Don't* fall into your inner child or fall apart in your habitual way.
- *Don't* lose concentration or break the mood.
- *Don't* disconnect from yourself or your partner.
- *Don't* give up.
- *Don't* judge or analyze.

- *Do* track each other carefully, keep eye contact as much as possible.
- *Do* keep physical contact, especially if you're using a blindfold.

- *Do* expose your contradictions, be open, be explicit.
- *Do* expose your secrets, focus on unresolved psychic material.
- *Do* push each other to the max, even slightly beyond your limits.
- *Do* hold on to your power, stay strong, yet always open and emotional.
- *Do* let yourself be taken apart, fall apart, descend into the void.
- *Do* let your emotions flow, wail if you need to, empty your heart.
- *Do* play-act fantasies, dreams, wild ideas, experiments.
- *Do* lots of touching, stay close physically and emotionally.
- *Do* stay connected, love each other, trust in your erotic union.

Your Arousal

In the Seeker, arousal is not an accident of chance. It is intentional, even if impulsive. Sometimes a shocking surprise can get the juices gushing, with the added tang of a burst of adrenaline.

Your Relationship with Your Body

Even though the Seeker emphasizes the mind, the playground of the Seeker is still the body. Be careful not to get too cerebral. The Seeker's mind focuses on drama, not calculation; tension, not planning. Like all tension, dramatic tension can be stored in the body—your body. So, find novel, creative ways to fill up your partner's body with intense erotic tension.

Your Erotic Fire

The furnace has become bigger as the erotic fire expands to include the mind. The mind is a strong erotic tool as witnessed by phone sex or sex on the Internet. The fire is both hotter and cooler. Hotter because the intensity is higher and pushed to the limit. Cooler because the vessel of the fire is larger. Imagine a fire in a bedroom versus the whole castle.

Your Orgasms

Let's continue, on the ever-popular subject of orgasms.

> Once I was inside her, Michelle held me tight. She clutched me hard, her fingernails digging into my back. I almost screamed, but then I realized I didn't feel a thing.
> I was almost in a trance state. I'd always felt like my mind was separate from my genitals. But this time, they were really connected, at least to a certain part of my mind—probably the same primal part our ancestors used a lot before we paved it over with grocery lists and phone numbers. Having my mind more connected to my crotch allowed me to lose my mind, let go of it. I was pure mind-body all in one.
> Our orgasmic energy climbed higher than I'd remembered before. The heat was more intense. I could totally surrender all of me into the flames of our lovemaking. When I finally starting coming, I cried. I held Michelle tightly and wept in her loving arms.
>
> — Michael

We sometimes call orgasms the crossroads of the soul. In that orgasmic moment, you can go in any direction. You have great freedom in changing who you are. The deeper we go into

Michael's trance-like state, the more malleable we can be in inner transformation.

It is ironic that the Seeker archetype uses the mind to intensify sexuality, but at the moment of orgasm it's the opposite: You can be more mindless than any other sexual archetype. Many lovers of the Seeker archetype call this state "going under." It is a supreme moment of what the French call "la petite mort" or the little death. Here you may "die" to your old ways, to be reborn into new, more life-giving values. At least, that is the possibility offered by the Seeker.

THE JOURNEY OF THE SEXUAL ARCHETYPES: DEEPENING YOUR SEXUALITY

So far on the journey, you have found your heart, your likes and dislikes, and your unstoppable passions. These are treasures indeed. Now as the Seeker, your *mind* is invited into the pantheon, to join the erotic dance. This is the second gateway of initiation, where the Self needs to die. You are at the threshold of the underworld where possessions and symbols of power must be left behind.

Like the goddess, Inanna, you must go naked now. You must meet with the demon face to face in the dark, in the cave, in a territory that is not yours. This is where your trial really happens, where you are tested, where you walk truly dangerous territory. If your heart has not been integrated, then you will be lost to the Shadow. You will be tested, not so much on a physical level, but in the inner realm here. You will meet the demons of shame, despair, self-deprecation, alienation, sorrow, betrayal and all their family, face to face. You, as the Seeker, will meet your limits, and enter the underworld realm of the Shadow. You will descend to Hades with Persephone.

This is the part of the journey when drama and tension enter the erotic space. Sexuality is still very physical, but no longer primarily physical. Your mind has become your chief erotic organ.

The play of energy here is the dynamic tension between power and surrender, between submission and mastery. You explore the underworld. It is the opportunity to be opened beyond the universe as you know it, to enter the mystery, to be cracked wide open. Here you are vulnerable, armed with no weapons, no defenses. And yet, miraculously, you survive. You thrive. You are welcomed in your nakedness to the archetypal world, to the realm of the seen and the unseen, always present at the same time. You are cleansed now, and ready to reveal and expose yourself fully, as you have never done before.

The Shadow

In a sense, the Seeker invites the Shadow. Unlike the other archetypes, the Shadow is an integral part of the archetypical dynamic. As e.e. cummings once said, the devil co-creates with God. Here, the Shadow co-creates with the Seeker. Above, we saw Michael confront his Shadow around menstrual blood. This confrontation with the Shadow helped transform Michael and deepen his relationship with Michelle.

However, in this section on the Shadow, we want to illustrate Shadow material which may not be welcome to your relationship. These are the bumps in the road which you will do better to avoid. Let's hear more from Michelle:

I'd never had Michael under my spell so completely before. Ooh, pure power! I really wanted to give Michael a run for his money. Part of me wanted to tease him so unmercifully he'd be begging me to have sex with him. I wanted him on his knees. I was remembering all the times he'd taken me for granted. Time to get even.

But that's not all. I wanted to rape him. Or at least humiliate him now that he was in my control. I was an evil witch. My anger was tangled up with being erotic and playful. But that's really how I felt.

Calling it a Shadow seemed like an understatement. More like I'd uncovered a mean-spirited side of mild-mannered Michelle. I didn't let myself go down that Shadow vortex. Neither did Michael.

— Michelle

LESSONS

I could tell Michelle was really getting into her new role as mistress. In fact, I was afraid she was getting a little too much into it. She might morph into her evil twin sister. We'd had our fights over the years, so I could imagine she might want to stick it to me. But I didn't want to rain on her parade either. I'd never seen her acting so boldly before. I was a little nervous. But her take-charge air was really hot. It really turned me on.

I was relieved when Michelle whispered in my ear that "red light" would be our "safe word" if I needed to stop the drama and bail out of the scene at any time for any reason.

When Michelle said that, things really shifted things for me. In that instant, I knew that I was safe—I could bail at any moment. More important, it was also a signal that we were inside one of Dr. Oona's ceremonial "spaces." I could dive in and surrender to whatever Michelle was cooking up. I wondered what that would be. But knowing Michelle, I knew it would be good!

— Michael

Part of the genius and paradox of the Seeker is enabling you to confront your biggest inner fears in perfect, loving safety—and getting juiced up in a new way in the process. Seems impossible, but people do it all the time. First and foremost, you need to have a deep level of trust between you. Hopefully, your play in the Innocent archetype helped strengthen this trust.

In addition to trust, here is a technical tip as well. Before you start your scene, discuss what people often call "safe words." These are words which wouldn't normally be part of your scene. You might choose "red light" to mean "stop," and "yellow light" to mean "slow down." And maybe "green light" to mean "don't worry, I'm fine."

You can make up your own words or just use these common signal words. The important thing is not to use common words like "no" and "yes." You may want to use these words as part of your scene. So, it would be very confusing if your partner said "no" but didn't actually want to halt the scene. So fasten your verbal seat belts, be safe, and have tons of erotic fun!

Your Turn

Here are some ideas to get started in the Seeker archetype:
- One dresses up powerfully, the other is naked
- Make your partner beg you for sex
- Blindfold your partner
- Tease your partner to the limit, use feathers, fingers, etc.
- Play out a fantasy, a drama
- Tie up your partner safely and sweetly
- Tell your partner, "You are mine, mine to please"
- Name a sexual situation where you encounter discomfort and dive into it

- Masturbate in front of your partner, hold the tension of being completely seen
- Start preparing a date two or three days beforehand, build expectation
- Put one of you in charge in all aspects of your life, the other surrendered for a day, then switch

Onward

I woke up in the morning with my eyes still wet. It wasn't just Michael who'd cried last night in his blindfolded bliss. I'd closed my eyes and sobbed through my last orgasm. They were jubilant tears washing away years of sadness, years of holding back, years of being afraid of being closer to Michael—and to myself.

The morning was warming up quickly. There were fields of summer wildflowers out our bedroom window. This is what it must have looked like when Persephone returned from the underworld. In that bright-eyed moment, I realized Michael and I had gone extra far and extra deep on last night's journey—maybe not all the way to Hades, but pretty close. I'd completely forgotten about that Sherlock Holmes video. We'd solved a few of our own mysteries instead. And that was a lot hotter!

I never would have guessed that confronting our inner fears would have been so incredibly sexy. There is something really sexy about courage.

*The word courage comes from the French word for "heart," **coeur**. That finally made sense now.*

We turned anxiety into an aphrodisiac. Now there's a tool I want to pack in my knapsack for the rest of the sexual archetypes mythic journey: sexual alchemy.

— Michelle

Welcome back from the underworld! It's springtime now. Let's celebrate Persephone's—and your—return from Hades back to the world of sunlight and wildflowers. We invite you to continue your journey of these nine sexual archetypes with the sunny-skied Revealer. Come!

CHAPTER SIX

Lighting the Way

THE REVEALER

"I really want to know you...
I really want to go with you.....I really want to show you..."
— The Beatles

When we saw Dr. Oona next, she congratulated us on sailing through four sexual archetypes already. She said we were now about to enter the fifth, the middle archetype, of the nine.

Dr. Oona said we'd spent the first four archetypes building and deepening our own personal sexual self-knowledge, confronting our own demons, getting confident in our likes and dislikes. Now, we were about ready to "give back" to others—and each other—in new, powerful ways. In the Revealer archetype we would be "tested" to see if we were "ready" for the last four sexual archetypes. Here we would gain charisma and personal sexual power.

Dr. Oona said the seemingly easiest things are often the hardest. In the Revealer, all we had to do was to tell each other what was really going on inside us—in complete hide-nothing, tantalizingly honest candid detail. That was it.

— Michelle

What juicy hidden secrets lie hidden in the hearts of Michelle and Michael? If they are like most couples, there is a treasure chest of private information ready to be unveiled. We'll get back to Michelle and Michael in a moment. First, let's invite the warm spotlight of Truth to bathe *you* and your partner right now.

Do you and your partner love pillow talk? Have you ever felt that rush of power when you stood up and said you're not ashamed to say you just plain love sex? Have you felt more intimate after your partner has just revealed a deep dark personal truth? Do you get that tingle of excitement when you're about to give your partner a peek at your own inner clandestine world? Do you like to tease and tantalize your partner with stories of naughty things you've done? Have you had more pleasure after you had the guts to say what you wanted your partner to do to you? Do you yearn to know your lover better, be closer, more merged into a single "us"?

Perhaps the Revealer is your "home" archetype. Or a great place to visit to deepen your relationship. Either way, this is the place of charisma and power in the world. Whether or not you are at home in the Revealer, it is a great place to learn to be a more powerful person in the world—in your work, in public speaking, in your community, and at home with your loved one.

We often like to say that sex is an undress rehearsal for all of life. Sex is a place where you can miraculously change who you are, become stronger, deepen your intentions and purpose in life. The Revealer, more than any of the other sexual archetypes, is a classroom for *all* of life. And what a fun classroom it is. Don't miss this sexual archetype!

Here's an initial glance at the sexual electricity of the Revealer:

- Available, tantalizing, alluring, teasingly playful, loving to tell stories

- Intimate, close, unafraid to meet eye-to-eye, an open book
- Regal, carrying the poise and stature of a queen or a king
- Candid, ruthlessly honest, speaking the unspeakable
- Successful, confident, projecting leadership, knowledgeable
- Intentional, thoughtful, open-minded, unprejudiced
- Powerful, charismatic, bigger than life, magnetic, strong in character
- Aware, alert, interested, drawing from a deep sense of knowing

When you're "inside" the Revealer archetype, you allow yourself to:

- Make love with your whole body, mind, emotions, and spirit
- Have sparkling fresh-eyed, explicit, speak-the-unspeakable pillow talk
- Tell all, tell your stories, your past loves, your present loves—everything
- Hear your partner's long-held inner secrets, and to hear them with new ears
- Claim your sexuality, your right to pleasure yourself
- Take your power and never give it away
- Love and be loved, make love with no reservations

For many of you, this may sound too good to be true. This may be the kind of intimacy that you always dreamed of, but couldn't imagine it existed on planet earth—at least not with mere mortals. Not so. You *can* discover and revel in the Revealer in your own love life. This archetype can be more erotic than any you've visited so far. And may demand more courage than any of the other sexual archetypes. But the challenge is well worth it. So do come with us.

SEX IN THE "TROPICAL SUN"

As with the other sexual archetypes, we have an island nickname for the Revealer, to help you tap into and daydream about this engaging archetype. Imagine...

You're a little blurry-eyed after emerging into the daylight after that trip to the underworld caves of the Seeker. You've learned a lot there. You are changed. You rub your eyes. The outer world has changed, too. Back in the sunshine, the sky is brighter, the ocean waves dazzle more, the flowers are more vivid, the trees stretch their limbs with more purpose now.

You and your sweetie are ready to just collapse on the beach. You fling off your clothes. The sand feels more gritty than you remember against your bare skin, but you savor the immediacy and genuineness of how it really feels. You curl up together, piling up sand into a makeshift pillow. The tropical sun highlights the feeling of total exposure of your body—and the rest of you as well: spirit, emotions, and mind. The openness you feel spills out of your eyes into your lover's.

As your bodies intertwine, deep secrets spill out through your whispering words, secrets made ready for the light of day. Your awkward words blend with your squirming bodies, undulating in the unedited glare of the tropical sun. You tell all. You make love to all of each other. You become one in ecstasy and in the beauty of your beloved tropical isle.

Sex in the Revealer

Meanwhile, let's see if Michelle and Michael are eager to share their inner truths with each other.

When we got home that evening, Michael and I were feeling a little cocky. We figured Dr. Oona's honesty assignment was for kindergarteners. We sensed some trouble up ahead, like the rumble of a waterfall when you're paddling on a river, but our blow-away successes with the first four archetypes buoyed our confidence.

We decided to celebrate, pausing for a well-earned halfway-point intermission in our archetypal exploration. Michael fixed a beautiful salmon dinner. After dinner, I got a fire going in the fireplace, and placed a whole ring of candles around the living room. Michael said it looked like an aboriginal ritual or something, where everyone chants around the campfire and they do human sacrifices.

I blurted out, "Let's do the honesty thing. No clothes. No secrets. No hiding anything."

We both stripped and faced each other, cross-legged on the floor, our bare skin glowing hot, bathed in the flames of the roaring fire. We held hands and looked into each other's eyes.

I'd never seen Michael do this before, but he offered a kind of prayer, as if we really were aboriginals. "I call upon the deities to witness our honesty, to protect us this night, and help us speak the unspeakable."

What secret gardens were we about to enter? What closets would we open this evening? Just the thought of it gave me goose bumps.

— Michelle

Luckily for Michael and Michelle, they didn't stay cocky and over-confident. On the contrary, their intuition kicked in just in time to mindfully prepare their space and put special, even prayerful, attention into the gravity of the "work" they were about to do.

We recommend that you too avoid leaping directly into indiscriminate honesty talk. You want a high-intensity burn, not an explosion. If you have something you want to tell or "confess" to your partner, at the very least ask if it's a good time right then. If not, agree on another time when you can really pay attention to each other—and can harness your sexuality as a powerful ally and catalyst in the process.

Let's continue with Michelle's and Michael's story. As we will see, sometimes a small afternoon event can energize a whole evening.

In this case, earlier in the afternoon, an attractive jogger caught Michelle's eye—or more importantly, Michelle's *staring* at the jogger caught Michael's eye. What were Michelle's inner thoughts as she looked dreamily at this gorgeous athlete in motion? Stay tuned.

Perhaps, you too think "ruthless honesty" can't be *that* hard or that erotic.

Truth-serum Sex

I could feel the heat of the fireplace inflaming my hands, drawing them toward Michelle's super-heated, eager skin, until we were lying down squirming, caressing each other all over. We could both feel the excitement. I don't know if it was lying on the rug in the wide open living room, or being inside the Revealer archetype, but I was feeling more naked and exposed than I had in years.

Michelle was also feeling more brazen. She lubed me up and just slid me inside her. I kissed her passionately. I blew in her ear and whispered, "So, what was going on in you when that hot jogger whished by you this afternoon?"

I could feel Michelle freeze up. Her vagina stopped moving, like cold stone. You always hear women telling us that we think with our dicks. Maybe women think with their vaginas. I probably would have gone limp, but Michelle barely missed a beat. She was back on line in a flash, as if she'd been preparing for this moment all afternoon. She squeezed me with her vagina's PC muscles.

"I admit it. I did like ogling at that college frat boy. He really turned me on. I'm not ashamed of my reaction." I was noticing I do like a strong, direct woman. I pumped Michelle a thank-you thrust. I loved the way she gasped. She tightened back in an explosive exhale. I wasn't sure who was in charge, our voices or our genitals.

Then came the zinger. "But it really wasn't about that lanky jogger. Sure, he was a babe, but he reminded me of a fantasy I've had for a long time, but have been terrified to tell you about. I thought you'd kill me. Maybe you will. It's about having one of those three-ways like you see in movies. Not with the jogger. I don't know him. But with a friend we could choose together. Someday, I'd love to bring just the right guy into our bed and have a ménage à trois. That's my speak-the-unspeakable truth, honey. Will you still make love with me, or even talk to me?"

I still was making love with Michelle. Right then. Didn't miss a thrust or a breath.

Normally, I would have fallen apart, I would have gone soft. I would have felt that she didn't love me anymore, that if she really loved me she wouldn't need some other man in our bed. I would have gotten mad.

Michelle was different too. Normally, she wouldn't have been able to stay moving and juicy through that kind of truth-telling, either. She would have gritted her teeth and turned to ice.

But being inside Michelle when we were talking was a whole new experience. We were both different.

— Michael

This may be the first time Michael and Michelle have been this forthright with each other—ever. They may have tried to broach a controversial subject or two at various times, but they probably found it hard to keep a hold on the thread. It's very hard to stay focused. Maybe Michael's and Michelle's normal habits are to try to talk intimately while lounging in the living room, or finishing up a meal at a table, or even sitting up in bed—instead of using their most powerful relationship "tool" of all, their white-hot sexuality.

However, once successfully begun, an honest conversation can keep going on like pulling a thread out of a sweater. More and more keeps coming and unraveling. In this case, it's important to go slowly, keep a mutually comfortable pace, and know when to take a break. Indeed, Michael may have some truths of his own to share. There will be plenty of time for that.

Speaking of breaks, let's take a short intermission to see what you've seen and can learn here. And we'll give you some tips for your own ecstatic truth-telling erotic pillow talk with your own sweetie.

First off, the Revealer is about the revealing moment itself, not the goal of getting to do new, exciting activities later. Sure, Michelle wants her threesome. But in the time-stopping moment of the Revealer, the focus is on staying with the thread of communication.

In your own lovemaking in this archetype, it may be very challenging to keep the erotic energy going. It's easy to go off course into soft and dry, instead of hard and wet. Don't be afraid to help each other out. Use sucking, lube, whatever it takes, to stay hard and wet. This is not heroics. It is connection and love. Brief intermissions are okay, too. Just try not to lose the moment. Don't run off to load the dishwasher. Try to stay in the moment, as if holding onto the same piece of yarn in common, together, for the whole evening.

You have probably noticed that it can be hard to "break the ice" bringing up a difficult subject to talk about. Michael wasn't too far off when he said Michelle's candles and roaring fire brought up the image of human sacrifices. Whoever brings up a taboo subject in a relationship can often feel like a human sacrifice if the conversation goes poorly. But these heroic, sacrificial deeds can open up a relationship, and infuse it with new material—at the right time.

The Revealer can be very tricky. Here are some things to remember to keep you on track.

- *Don't* waver, equivocate, hesitate, waffle.
- *Don't* be pigheaded, unilateral, single-minded.
- *Don't* grit your teeth. Don't say "this is how it is, deal with it."
- *Don't* collapse, dump, whine. Don't let your emotions take over.
- *Don't* be cold, distant, controlling, manipulative.
- *Don't* disconnect from your body and your heart, don't freeze up.
- *Don't* be judgmental, know-it-all, holier-than-thou.

- *Don't* be a spectator. Don't hide behind the camera lens.
- *Don't* worry about the "small stuff" like cleaning up the dishes after dinner.
- *Don't* take yourself or your relationship too seriously.
- *Don't* jump into truth telling unless the time is right and you are prepared.
- *Don't* try to tell too much truth in one night. Pace yourselves.

- *Do* be erotic, lusty, eager, clear-channel, sexual, skin-touching.
- *Do* reveal yourself, tell all. Listen to all from your partner.
- *Do* tell your truth as a story, build up a little suspense, tease and tantalize.
- *Do* stay engaged, in relationship, in negotiation, in give and take, in physical contact.
- *Do* remember that it's your relationship. It doesn't belong to anyone else.
- *Do* celebrate your will, your heart's desires, your hungers, your fantasies.
- *Do* be spontaneous, imaginative, creative, open-minded, light.
- *Do* be a clear beacon, forthright, unashamed, unabashed, unafraid.
- *Do* be detailed, explicit. Indulge in your erotic imagination.
- *Do* be discriminating, use good timing, there's no rush, "unfold" the truth.
- *Do* hold any tension between you and your partner as embodied sexual tension.

- *Do* communicate through your bodies and genitals, not just with words.
- *Do* touch, adore, be compassionate, appreciate, caress, lust after your partner.

Imagine that you are the queen or king of a vast realm. Who you are and what you think about is divinely right. Your royal subjects want to hear from you, be inspired by your vision and leadership. You communicate well to them. You are not apologetic. Neither are you blustering or belligerent. There's no need to be. You are powerful. You are an example of goodness and beauty. You are compassionate. Find that king or queen within you. Make love to your royal beloved.

In your realm there are many conflicting voices. As the king or queen you are wise enough not to choose sides. You are inclusive. You hold the both-and of *E Pluribus Unum:* "Out of many there is one."

SEX IN THE BOTH-AND

It was so erotic to tell Michael my secret fantasy. And it was even more erotic to ride through the abyss of scary truth, and stay hot and connected. Michael stayed hard, too. I just about came. I never would have expected any of that.

A big load slid off my chest. Feeling lighter was a sexy feeling, too. Then I wondered what Michael might have been hiding from me all these years. What bombshells did he have stashed away?

Michael surprised me when he said he couldn't really think of any big secrets. He had his own zinger, though. Never underestimate Michael. He said that part of him did think the idea of a three-way was just plain sick. But that was just part of him. What blew me away was when he murmured quietly that another part of him actually got *turned on when I shared my fantasy. To be honest with himself—and me—he had to admit that the idea of having another man sucking on my breasts made him very hard.*

When he said that, my body whizzed ahead of my mind and went into a wild gyration of ecstatic twisting and undulating, writhing, and thrashing. Michael just moaned and rode me harder, and held me tightly in his arms.

— Michelle

The sexual tension and electricity of the Revealer often comes from truths which may be hidden, even from yourself. You may carry lots of conflicting truths within you. That's fine. That's normal. In fact, it's unavoidable. In Michael's case, his genitals didn't agree with his beliefs about monogamy. He was split. That's normal.

The genius of the Revealer is that he doesn't need to be embarrassed about his contradictions or try to resolve them. He and Michelle can hold this "both-and" truth-tension, and enjoy Michael for his deep humanity and the complex human he is.

You too, no doubt, have lots of contradictions swimming around inside you. Be as open to your partner about them as you can—in good time. Hold them in your body. Feel the tingle of their jagged edges. Harness them in your sex play. Rejoice in both sides of a contradiction. Let yourselves live your lives both ways.

Don't force yourselves to choose sides prematurely. Rather, honor both sides as Michael does. He doesn't abdicate his values by admitting that a ménage à trois actually—if the truth be told—turns him on. Michelle, on the other hand, doesn't jump on this as an opportunity to pressure him into inviting a new playmate into their bedroom. They hold the tension in their midst. And they sexualize it by going with it, not breaking the mood to disagree or point out the contradictions.

Remember, sex is ultimately more about yes's than no's. As we like to say, "The universe knows no no's."

Speaking of yes's, this brings us to an always favorite topic, orgasms!

Your Orgasms

I had never talked so much during sex. But this kind of talking was pretty steamy. I was flying pretty high because of all this true-confessions chat.

Then Michael whispered in my ear to imagine that there was another man in the room right now. I couldn't believe he really said that. But he did.

My imagination sped off like a Corvette on an autobahn with no speed limits. My body was in hot pursuit, flying into a frenzy of ever faster acceleration until I really did feel two men with me.

Michael had taken my fantasy, and run with it. As he slid his hard rod inside me, I felt completely ravished and accepted.

Michael was just as hot. He grabbed me and screamed as we both exploded and collapsed into each other's sweaty arms. My long-kept secret was vaporized in a single flame of cleansing orgasm. We were free to be who we really are with each other.

— Michelle

Here's a challenge for you. Try to take your contradictions and inner conflicts into orgasm. This is the place where *all* is possible and *all* is included. Even though you may have lots of inner conflicts, in the flash of orgasm, you can experience the grace of the moment, the patience of the universe.

You can also savor the moment to taste new possibilities of your future, that you can indeed change. You can begin to take on new values. Follow your sexuality as a teacher. Don't blindly follow your erotic juices, but do use sex as a way to renew your values—your values, no one else's!

And, most importantly, be patient and kind with yourselves. You will have steps forward and steps back. Sometimes an expansive breakthrough will be followed the very next morning by a fearful contraction of "you fantasize about what?" When that happens, remember to keep breathing and agree to wait to dive into the tangle of feelings until you can set aside some protected time together. Even then, you will have your inevitable ups and downs.

THE JOURNEY OF THE SEXUAL ARCHETYPES: EXPOSED SEXUALITY

The Revealer is a time of integration and understanding, a pause after inhaling the first four archetypes. The Revealer pauses to understand the meaning of it all, the meaning of the erotic fire, the meaning of our sexual nature, the meaning of the rules and agreements that we have in our sexuality.

After encountering the underworld, you are heralded as Kings and Queens. You have acquired great knowledge. It is the completion of the integration of the mind, begun with the Seeker.

The Revealer's task is to understand the present matrix, discern the truth, and render that revelation to your lover. Here you become conscious. In making the invisible visible, the unspeakable spoken, Persephone returns from the underworld as Queen. The Revealer transforms the painful past into the light of day. It is the place of integration and knowledge and the gateway from the personal to the collective, the transition from being wrapped up in your own story, on to the freedom and the availability to giving to or serving others.

Moreover, the task of the Revealer is to revisit all agreements that you have around sexuality and relationship. Did you give yourself away in your marriage? Did you give away your power saying yes to an open marriage? Did you give yourself away when agreeing to monogamy?

The Revealer lives in the realm of the agreement, intentional and implicit, for good and for ill: the husband who expects sex on demand; the wife who "does it" in exchange for family and security; prostitutes and their johns; games of truth or dare; the ability to stop and look at consequences or to put on a condom; responsible thought and reaction; rationality and rationales; the King and Queen who declare their power.

Through the centuries people have traded sex and marriage to access power, wealth, or security. The Revealer takes many forms, many portrayed in movies. In *The Thomas Crown Affair*, Pierce Brosnan uses his mind for a game of cat and mouse which amplifies the erotic game. Mickey Rourke in the movie *Wild Orchid* embodies the Revealer by naming the unspeakable about sexuality. In *Indecent Proposal*, Robert Redford consciously contracts for sex and the calculated game of power. The woman? She accepts the contract, not only for the money, but also to get closer to power. In *Dangerous Beauty*, Veronica's livelihood is assured by the web of sexual contracts she has carefully chosen.

The quintessential movie highlighting the Revealer is Stanley Kubrick's *Eyes Wide Shut*. Here Nicole Kidman and Tom Cruise struggle with the abiding question, should they tell their true love *everything*, not just deeds but what they are thinking too?

Don't let the unrealistic orgy scenes distract you from the central thought-provoking theme.

The Revealer is deeply present in our sexuality even if often not acknowledged as such. Agreements about safe sex are made from the Revealer. The commitment to a relationship that will endure difficult times is held by this archetype, by the power of the choice and the will. The Revealer is the adult aspect of the self, the one that manages the kingdom, the business, and keeps things in order. So as to be able to dive deeply in the underworld and to heaven, so you can surrender to the waves of desire, letting Aphrodite take you over, you need a character in your psyche that makes sure that your house stays in order. It is the way that your boundaries get created and kept. The Revealer protects you through the use of the will and conscious choice.

In this archetype, partners may spontaneously reveal private, secret information about themselves. The Revealer is empowered by the very revelation. Both partners will feel their relationship deepening as a result of it. It is a time of taking risks to the end of a greater self and mutual integrity. There is a desire to stand up for yourself. And there is something in the acceptance of the unspeakable truth that is deeply erotic.

How to Get Started

As with many of our archetypes, it can be difficult to kick start the mood, getting you feeling like you're inside the archetype. For the Revealer, you will want to bring with you lessons from the previous four archetypes. Here's a quick list for your toolbox. From each sexual archetype:

The Innocent...   *brings trust, understanding, fun, and playfulness*

The Adventurer... *brings courage, excitement, and venturesome boldness*

The Sensualist... *brings lust and sexual brazenness*

The Seeker... *brings self-knowledge and self-acceptance*

Let's see how Michelle and Michael use these tools to set the stage for the wonderful sexual connection you read about earlier.

Setting the Stage

Michelle and I were both feeling rather bold when we left Dr. Oona's. We even decided to walk home a new way. The sky was clear, the air was warm and still. I was mulling over our latest puzzling assignment. Something to do with honesty. Seemed like it would be a snap.

Michelle was the first to talk. "It can't be that hard to be totally, scrupulously honest. Let's try it."

I thought out loud, "Is it okay to ask questions, too?"

Michelle said, "Why not?"

We walked for a while not talking much at all. I think Michelle was doing the same thing I was doing, pawing through the insides of her brain thinking there really wasn't much to hide. Just then a cute athletic college frat boy jogged by in a tank top and thin running shorts with about two square inches of material. I noticed that Michelle's eyes were tracking him like NASA tracking a Mars space probe.

I couldn't resist a playful question. "So what goes through your mind when you see that jogger? No, I've got a better question, what goes through your body when you see him?"

Michelle was not done watching him disappear in the distance when I pounced with that winning question. I figured I'd nailed her.

What was she going to say? Actually, I was really curious what goes on inside her. I'd never asked before, probably because I didn't want to know.

She said, "I'll tell you, but you've got to answer the very same question. Turn about is fair play. I noticed you were staring at him too."

Looks like we really were going home a new way, all right. I was already feeling lost.

— Michael

An important key to the Revealer is discovering what new "material" to chew on, finding grist for the sexual mill. Be on the lookout for those situations where you have a pattern of being silent, maybe because you didn't want to get into areas which might pick a fight.

Don't worry if your material is different from Michael's and Michelle's. You have your own issues and hot buttons.

Once you find this "gold mine" of sensitive material, turn on the retro jets, reverse the thrusters on your engines. Slow down. Stay connected. And let your heart thump a bit.

Casting the Stars

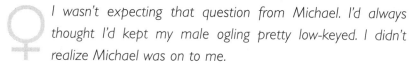 *I wasn't expecting that question from Michael. I'd always thought I'd kept my male ogling pretty low-keyed. I didn't realize Michael was on to me.*

What should I tell Michael? At first I told myself that looking at cute guys was really no big deal for me. It was no different from looking at that blossoming peach tree over there or a pretty painting at the museum. I was about to say that to Michael, when realized that Michael and I were at a major crossroads. I needed to take Dr. Oona's truth serum and just go for it, pedal to

the metal. That go-for-it feeling reminded me of some of the other sexual archetypes. Being alive and fully awake. I eased my foot onto the gas pedal. I had a last fleeting thought that things would never be the same again.

Michael saved me at this point. He understood that we were in for something big. He said, "This could get pretty intense. I think we should wait to talk about this till we get home and can really pay attention to what we're saying to each other."

Michael was right.

My heart was thumping, but I was glad to have more time to collect my thoughts and figure out how that jogger managed to frazzle my whole nervous system.

— Michelle

Notice how Michael and Michelle save divulging their sensitive material until later when they can be more connected, and physically closer. Try doing this yourself. Think of this "later time" as a kind of "ceremony"—sexual ceremony. Give it its special due, its fullness of time.

The Shadow

Playing the Revealer can feel like walking a tightrope sometimes. You might feel pretty precarious, just about to fall off into the abyss of an argument at any time. Michelle describes some of the most common pitfalls below.

Michael and I crashed into the Shadow right out of the box with our initial cockiness. We started out in the Revealer with a foolhardy level of overconfidence. In retrospect, we were flying too close to the sun. We wavered between the hubris of thinking we didn't have any secrets, and dismissing the pain locked in the secrets we did have. Either way, if we'd kept charging ahead, we would have ended up either in a big crunch or a big freeze.

But we had the good sense to wait till we could set up an intimate space for our pillow talk. It was worth the delay. That was the hottest pillow talk.

Another place I hit the Shadow was when I started telling Michael about wanting to do a ménage à trois someday. When he didn't kill me—rather kept the sexual steam blasting—I was tempted to seize this golden moment and get him to agree to one soon. But I realized that just telling him about my fantasy was a mega accomplishment for us.

The other big Shadow zone was when Michael said that part of him thought a three-way was sick, but another part of him got really turned on by the idea. I was tempted to point out that he was contradicting himself. Of course, he's not dumb. He could see that himself.

In the juice of the Revealer, I realized that Michael's contradictions are part of his charm and allure. And sex appeal. I'd never understood that before.

— Michelle

We face directly into our own Shadow material here in the Revealer. So be patient with yourself. The Revealer is a rich mother lode of psychic and relationship material. No need to mine it all in a day. It will take years. So enjoy it, discover it, and let your sensuality flow.

You have been to the underworld and faced your own inner conflicts. You know who you are now. The Shadow aspect of the Revealer can manifest when you offer your mate too much of this newfound insight all at once, or reveal secrets your mate isn't prepared to hear just yet. The Revealer can be a pivotal relationship-breaker or a relationship-maker. So be careful.

Another aspect of the Shadow of the Revealer is to be so in control of your emotions that your lust is suppressed. This Shadow will show up in the armoring of your body and your lack of ease and flow. The Revealer Shadow is rather a stern character, and not very engaging as a lover. The poetry is missing.

The Shadow is often experienced as a disconnection from the body and hence the difficulties in letting go into orgasmic chaos. Your partner, frozen in the Shadow of the Revealer, will tell you everything she or he likes and what turns them on but will not be able to feel it strongly.

The Shadow of the Revealer is disconnectedness, communication that lacks compassion, in bluntly spoken truth that has not been integrated in the heart, and in deal-making or business-for-sex arrangements if it diminishes one of the partners. The head-without-heart separation from the instinctual or improvisational is found in the Shadow of the Revealer. The immature Revealer is full of mentally generated stress, mechanical ideas without passion, or sex from a how-to book. Intimacy can be a struggle for those who live primarily in this archetype.

LESSONS

The Revealer, after the journey into the underworld, gets the robe of jewels, the wisdom and the power. Here we become king and queen, not because we inherited it or bought it, but because we *earned* it, and because we *claim* it. It is the power that comes from wisdom, from self-knowledge and the knowledge of your relation to what is larger than the self.

To claim truth, the Revealer must be self-expressed and clear, articulate and compassionate. Truth without compassion is brutal and ruthless. The gift of the Revealer is awakening to your life purpose and power, claiming your life and taking responsibility for it. In order to do this, you have to show up. This is the gift of clarity and commitment. The Revealer encourages relationships where power exists and is part of the connection of the erotic dance. Power is the charm and the curse of the Revealer, the attraction and the contraction.

Good sexuality is a dance between tension and union, merging and separation. The Revealer is an exploration of the tension of differentiation, of being individuated and standing in your own power. Letting yourself feel both power and Eros in the same intimate moment where a conflicting experience brings up discomfort. The ability to hold the paradoxes of life in the same moment is the gift of the Revealer, the opening to a sense of freedom of being.

Your Turn

Here are some ideas to get started in the Revealer archetype:

- Play "Truth or Dare"
- Tell your partner something scandalous you'd like to do
- Write an erotic story
- Tell your partner that you want, desire, hunger for him or her
- Look at the agreements—spoken and unspoken—you have made around sex
- Confront your fears, challenge your preconceptions and normal habits; speak the deeper truths you are afraid to share

Onward

Whereas previously you played with power, now you *have* the power of hard-won experience and courageously spoken truth. It is not yet heaven, but the sojourner can anticipate many wonders on the horizon. The empathy and humility of understanding yourself leads us to bring that wisdom to others. And so, you continue on your journey, already halfway around the circle now.

You hear the sound of thunder in the distance. Is a storm coming?

CHAPTER SEVEN

Mastering the Fire

THE MAGICIAN

"Be not forgetful to entertain strangers,
for thereby some have entertained angels unawares."
— Hebrews 13:2

Oona said our assignment for the Magician would be to dive into the hottest embers of the fire, and to embody what we most fear. I immediately started panicking that we had to grab some greasy guy and drag him into our bedroom to help "embody" Michelle's ménage à trois kinky fantasy. I was about ready to tell her where she could put her sexual archetypes.

But this assignment was just for the two of us. Our challenge was to use our imaginations and our sexuality to heat up our fears to the melting point. Then, like red-hot iron, we could forge our swords into scepters, our trepidations into titillations.

It sounded too good to be true, but if we could use sex to burn through our sexual fears, I was all set to sign up. I had a sense that Michelle and I were in for a wild ride on this archetype.

— Michael

It looks like Michelle and Michael have really opened Pandora's box this time! We'll return to their story soon to see how they handle one of the biggest sticking points of all relationships, unbounded sexuality.

But first, let's see where *your* life and relationship can use some magical fairy dust. It might have nothing to do with Michael's worries over his partner's lusts. It might be something personal, or about your body. Lots of things have hurt us over the years. It's time to be healed. And your lover can be your most gifted healer.

Have you ever felt that your love could heal other people? Have you ever made a big breakthrough in your relationship and watched your partner's eyes grow brighter? Have you gone to the perfect ocean beach and noticed that the sparkles in the ocean waves were reflected in your lover's misty eyes? Do you have some issue which comes around again and again like a persistent mosquito on a summer night? Do you yearn to get more sleep at night instead of arguing over that affair you now wished you'd kept mum about?

Do you sometimes feel that your eyes and your love are a mirror where your partner can see your divine nature? Do you sometimes connect to a deeper knowledge of the sexual nature and feel that your hands, body, soul are of service to your Beloved? Have there been times when you trusted in the universe and you were rewarded? Have you had such intense sex that you felt all your molecules got rearranged?

You might be surprised. The Magician just might be your "home" archetype. If not, please plan on vacationing to this magical land whenever you can. The Magician is the great healer for your relationship. With this archetype you can miraculously change the direction of your relationship. Invite the Magician when you start going into a skid. When you get stuck, the Magician can help you navigate out of the mud.

Here's a quick glance at the sexual electricity of the Magician:

- Complete connection/openness, presence, availability
- Total embodiment
- Fearless and wise
- Serene, totally accepting
- Sexually powerful, masterful, deft, nimble
- Healing, life changing, transforming, renewing
- Teaching each other with a gentle hands-on presence
- Tapped into the deep sexual aquifers of the soul
- Otherworldly, enchanted, dream-like, unfettered, flowing
- Fairy tale–like, showered with pixie dust
- Selfless, no need to be yourself, free to be anyone
- Conscious, insightful, prepared, careful, knowing
- Ability to go anywhere, to be with anyone
- Imaginative, creative, inventive, surprising, even shocking
- Wide open to new sexual territory, no hesitation
- Trustful of the universe, bigger than you think you are
- Open to being transformed, your "molecules rearranged"
- Forgiving, caring, adoring, loving, connected, touching

When you're inside the Magician archetype, you are:

- Connected to yourself
- Free of your own limitations and fears
- Changed, unstuck, back in the groove, transformed, renewed
- Powerful, effective, free, open to change
- Engaged, amused, entertained, sourced
- Effortlessly in control of what needs to be controlled, nothing more
- Aligned with the deities themselves

- In the "Zone," surfing in the waves of the universe
- Connected not just to each other, but to the "all"
- Pretty much open to anything, a land of acceptance
- Aware of the process, free of goals

For some of you, the Magician may sound scary. Tinkering with your relationship may not seem worth drilling down into the magma of deep-seated core issues. You may get a new volcano spurting molten lava onto the living room rug. What a mess to clean up...

For others, the Magician is a dream come true. Perhaps you want to change your relationship and each other, too. But there are so many pitfalls. You're wary of turning your partner into a "project." And yet, maybe you are tired of repetitively crashing into the same old hurts and phobias over and over again. Here we entreat you to have faith—faith in the universe and faith in yourselves. We won't try to sugarcoat this archetype, though. The rewards of the Magician are galactic in size. To be changed is to encounter *spirit*, the life-force breath energy itself—which is sexuality and its creative generative power in the deepest sense.

SEX AT THE "TRIBAL DANCE"

Our snapshot for the Magician conjures up images of naked ancestors dancing ecstatically around a fire in a trance state, in a kind of benign possession.

Daydream this image:

You have spent the day basking in the tropical sun, confessing your deepest secrets to your lover in the glare of the screaming blue sky. And hearing your partner's tell-all to you, too. You have unearthed more than perhaps you wanted to mine out of your lover's inner private world, but you hold this new knowledge as if you are holding a newfound seashell, lovingly brushing the dried sand off of it.

Now the sun is sliding lower toward the seaward horizon. The sky is growing cloudy and tempestuous. Just then, you hear the enchanting call of deep resonant drums and shrill chanting, wafting through the jungle's verdant fronds. You follow your ears, making your way through the dense, moist vegetation, finally emerging into a clearing with a fire burning and smoking at its center.

You spot a pile of costumes and paint nearby. You and your lover instinctively know what to wear, and what designs to adorn on your naked skin, what personae to take on. Your bodies are already moving and animated by the music and the otherworldly drumbeat.

In your new forms, the two of you dance yourselves into a wild frenzy, losing yourselves, becoming your new characters. Your eyes meet as new people you've never known before. You continue gyrating, touching more now, eyes locked in a laser embrace.

The music crescendos until your mind is no more. You collapse together, bright eyed, bodies wrapped in skin-to-painted-skin union. You make love as never before, your bodies glowing as red-hot ingots forged by the fire of your pure life energies. You are changed, renewed, remade, reformed—in love in a new way you have never known before.

Trouble in the Sexual Jungle

Sorry to say, it's not always that simple and straightforward to find the clearing for the ecstatic, mind-losing Tribal Dance of the Magician. You may have to search harder than you might think.

As we will see with Michelle and Michael, it will take them a few more twists and turns to make it through their jungle of raw feelings to get to their own ecstatic Tribal Dance. But they will make it. More importantly, you too will make it! But it may be a slog. So be persistent!

Let's join Michelle and Michael as they prepare for their Tribal Dance. As we were saying, it looks like they're not quite ready to tango just yet.

Michael wants the very best for Michelle, including helping her live out her heart's delight. Michael is even a bit curious, even excited, about what one of Michelle's ménages would actually look like. But mostly, Michael is terrified of Michelle carrying out her fantasy and sharing sexual intimacy with another person.

Michelle is feeling very misunderstood. She feels betrayed and punished by Michael for speaking out her inner truth. She's also feeling strong. No one can ever take away from her what she said about the deliciousness of her fantasy. It was the real, authentic Michelle. So Michael will just have to deal with it.

As we join Michelle and Michael, they are still angry at each other and stuck. They are getting weary and feeling hopeless—light years away from feeling sexy. Their bodies are contracted and looking fortified. Their faces are hard and worn.

With their energy leaving their bodies like rain draining down gutters, Michelle dials the phone and asks for an emergency evening session with Oona.

We arrived at Oona's office soaked from another squall. We told her about the quagmire Michelle and I had been slogging through all afternoon, and how we felt angry and so totally hopeless. And how we felt about as erotic as the mud still stuck to the bottom of our shoes.

Oona said we needed to dive right into the middle of our fire, whatever it was.

For me, my "fire" was the "other" phantom guy in Michelle's ménage fantasy. Even though this guy didn't really exist, he was as real as day for me.

Oona said that if I were so terrified of some "other guy," then we should make that "ground zero" for the Magician. In our sex play, I should go ahead and "become" the other guy—magically switch places. In real life you usually have to be yourself, but in sex, especially in the Magician sexual archetype, you can be anyone you want. Pick what threatens you the most, and be that— or him in my case.

That did sound like going directly into the fire. I could feel the flames already beginning to singe my neurons. On the bright side, I could also feel some new heat in my loins.

Oona suggested we imagine we were sent by magic carpet to some ancient South Seas Tribal Dance, where sex was always magical. Especially in the Magician archetype.

— Michael

Sex in the Magician: Heading Off Your Own Tribal Dance

When you plan your healing times with the Magician, think about how you can change your patterns for the evening. Think wild cards. Think outlandish ideas. Think vivid images. And don't be afraid to play-act the images once you hatch them. Remember, sex calls *all* of us to play, our minds, emotions, bodies—and with full passion!

For example, let's say your partner had a bad first sexual experience back in her teenage years. Before you met the Magician, you might have said, "Oh, I'm sorry to hear that, honey. Cheer up. It's long gone now." Forget all that in the Magician. Here you can recreate the experience itself, right in the safety of your bedroom. And you get to be the guy who's going to make what's wrong, right! Your lucky night.

Now here comes the trick. You'll want to recreate the original scene as authentically as you can, just up to the point where your partner is starting to relive it. Now here's the creative fork in the road. This time, you get to give the experience a happily-ever-after ending. Your partner gets to find the crossroads where power and healing take place, where the past is burned up with the fire of presence.

This is alchemy. You are turning lead into gold, bad past experiences into happy present experiences, with your present partner. As you become more familiar with the Magician, you will become more fluent in coming up with lots of creative ways to heal yourselves. We'll give you more ideas as we continue.

Back to Michelle and Michael.

♀ *Michael and I got home and didn't even pause to bring in the newspaper, or even turn on the lights when we got inside. Moonlight streamed in the windows anyway. The house was warm and enveloping, about a million miles from the chilled downpours of the day. I hardly remembered who I was.*

Without saying a word, we crept our way to our bedroom, imagining we were inching our way through dense jungle vegetation. When we got there, we lit a circle of candles, changed into silk robes, and faced each other on the bed.

I was about to open my mouth when this man gently put his hand on my lips, and whispered, "I've been waiting for you. My name is Bob." I blinked. Was I in a dream?

— Michelle

No, this is not a dream. Well, not exactly. Michelle and Michael have finally accepted the invitation of the Magician. In this case, Michael has taken Oona's suggestion, and gone into the fire of his worst fear of the moment: Michelle having sex with another person. Michael has become "Bob"—at least for the moment. Of course, there is no Bob, or anyone else other than Michelle in the bedroom. Michael is play-acting Bob for this "scene" only.

You will, no doubt, have your own repertoire of worst fears. Track them down like wild animals. Capture them in your imaginations. Use their energy to light the fire of the Magician. Master the fire.

Sex at the "Tribal Dance," Take Two

It took me a few seconds to jump into the mind-bend of being "Bob" in our bedroom. But the mindset clicked in amazingly fast. In fact, after a couple of seconds, my mind was completely switched off, and I was just doing it. It was almost scary how easily I slipped into this non-existent Bob.

The anger and accusations of the day were a million miles from our South Seas ring of flickering candles. I looked into Michelle's eyes and I heard her say, "Bob, it's you. I want you." The Tribal Dance had begun!

As Bob, I took Michelle's hand gently, and felt Michael somehow also in the room. I think he was watching us intently. I slid Michelle's robe off her glistening shoulders. It dropped on the bed revealing her breasts. We lay back in the bed together, our hands exploring each other's flesh.

I kissed Michelle's arms and neck and face. She relaxed back, drinking in my touch.

Michelle's fingers teased my sensitive thighs, and drew circles on my chest. She seemed to inhale the quivering flesh of two men so effortlessly. It took my breath away.

Just then she kissed me passionately, and in that flash of an instant, some deep unspoken message passed through her lips into mine. In a single electric jolt, I got a deep, deep pleasure-filled knowing that Michelle was truly loving in her heart, the delight of this almost-real ménage à trois. She was beautiful.

— Michael

The Magician in Michael is transforming his aesthetics. Whereas earlier in the afternoon, the thought of Michelle in her ménage was repulsive, now Michael experiences the idea of a ménage, through Michelle, as beautiful—pleasurable. This is sexual alchemy.

Notice "Bob" doesn't dive into intercourse right away. Bob stays in character (as Michael imagines it). After all, this is the first time Bob has ever been in bed with Michelle. We see that the "Bob" in Michael's imagination proceeds slowly. That's good information for both Michelle and Michael. In other words, Michael is exploring his level of comfort with what a real "Bob" might do. Michael's old sensational picture of a ménage is turning into more detailed, "hands-on" *understanding*.

Also, remember that this is not a rehearsal for "the real ménage" to come. Not at all. This is a healing for Michael's anxieties on the subject. Whether they ever truly act out this fantasy later is a totally different issue. For now, they just need to be able to include Michelle's fantasy inside their "circle" of conversation and lovemaking, and not get "triggered" so easily. They are increasing the size of the "circle" of their relationship, enlarging their mutual space, freeing up fears into available energy.

In your love life, don't expect this transformation quite this rapidly. In fact, don't expect it at all. It is a miracle. Change is always a miracle, especially change in aesthetics, change in what we find beautiful. Be patient. Michael and Michelle are pretty quick to jump into their turn-the-tables "dream" on the first try. It may take you much longer. But you never know... When you put your fears aside, it's amazing how miracles begin appearing in your life.

Your Orgasms

Orgasms are not an important element of the Magician per se. It really depends on the particular magical healing you are doing. You might stay with the fresh exploration and kissing that Bob and Michelle were savoring. Or your scene might lead in different directions which might totally surprise you.

On this night, it so happens that Michael is not the only one desiring some magic. A few weeks ago, Michelle read about so-called "G-spots." She has always enjoyed intercourse with Michael, but began wondering if she could have even more intense vaginal orgasms by stimulating a certain sensitive part of her vagina that an article described.

Michelle tentatively broached the delicate subject with Michael. But he said that looking for her G-spot seemed kind of kooky. Plus it seemed more like school homework than romantic lovemaking to Michael. He said it was a turnoff for him. Michelle was extremely disappointed. Naturally, she really wanted to know her body and her sexual response better. Maybe Michael was offended deep down that his lovemaking wasn't good enough. In any case, they were silently stuck here.

Now this evening, with the Magician in the room, things were different. Michael's mind has been hijacked and expanded. Let's continue with our courageous couple and see where their love scene goes under the stars of the wild-card Magician.

♀ *"Bob" was so attentive and exquisitely sensitive. He knew just how to touch me. He had a slow, tender way of kissing me that made me almost come on the spot. But, before I could respond, "Bob" did something Michael had never ever done before. He traced his fingers down from my neck to my thighs, made a large circle around my nether lips, and then paused. As my body opened he lubed up his right hand and gently parted my labia and entered me with two fingers. I felt a warm tingle course through my core. He slid his fingers in deeply and curved them up slightly. All the while he was looking me straight in the eye. Bob had read that article on G-spots I'd left around for Michael. He knew just what to do. He moved his fingers just a smidge. I could feel him pressing gently on the roof of my vagina.*

I felt new waves of pleasure, tears, laughter and sorrow wash over me, moving from one emotion to the next. "Bob," attentive to each emotion, was holding me in his gaze as a precious treasure, letting emotions pass, pure energy release from a space and a time mysterious even to me.

There was a surge of high-voltage electricity. Then he hit the jackpot. My brain circuits frizzed into infinity. Bob's fingers moved faster. Then slower for a moment, caressing my clit. Then back on my G-spot. "Yes", I screamed, "Bob!"

— Michelle

If you've always been "yourself" in the bedroom, you are in for a treat with the Magician. You can be anyone now. Remember though, the Magician is not just fun. As we saw above, this archetype can transform your relationship, change it at its core. If that's not magic, what is?

Michelle and Michael also showed that the Magician is not a stroll in the park either. It can be stormy out there. You may need an umbrella. Here are some additional tips to help you with this often challenging, tempestuous archetype:

- *Don't* fear.
- *Don't* get caught in each others' drama, sorrow, or pain; don't feed it.
- *Don't* manage and manipulate, you each have to heal yourselves.
- *Don't* try to fix anything, your partner is not broken.
- *Don't* be the know-it-all.
- *Don't* forget yourself.
- *Don't* become a technician.

- *Do* be attentive and inquisitive.
- *Do* be open to what is present right then.
- *Do* be open to healing, teaching, transforming who you are.
- *Do* put your own personal "stuff" aside.
- *Do* be self-confident, self-assured.
- *Do* track your partners every eye movement and twitch, be attentive.
- *Do* prepare well, call in your "higher" side, your higher values.
- *Do* have no shame around sexuality, deal with issues beforehand if you can.

- *Do* be spacious, inclusive, understanding, responsible.
- *Do* be of service, give away your treasures.
- *Do* always stay connected to your own pleasure, your preferences, your own sexuality.
- *Do* speak the truth, do not protect your partner from the truth.
- *Do* see power and possibility in your partner, be a "mirror" of their best side.
- *Do* be loving, caring, adoring, lustful, erotic, sexy.

Your Arousal

In the Magician, arousal comes more from caring, serving, and giving away, than from lust and hunger. Here sex is a giveaway, an honoring of your partner. Stay connected to your lust, but don't let it drive you off course.

Your Erotic Fire

This is the archetype of "mastering the fire." Here you can channel and direct the fire for the good of your partner and your relationship. You can use the fire to melt down hard stuck places in your partnership.

In the Magician, you can learn that your erotic fire has no fixed pattern. Eros is *pure energy* here. For example, you can use your sexuality to ignite a secret heart's-desire daydream. At the same time, you can use the same sexual juice to burn up a nightmare. Or this pure light sexuality can be used to train yourselves on a new anatomical hot button, like your G-spot. You can even use your erotic fire to infuse your dinnertime conversation. Sexuality here is like a Swiss Army Knife. The possibilities are unlimited.

Your Relationship with Your Body

Magicians are maestros at conducting the symphony of the erotic fire. They can play their lovers like a Stradivarius, and can help their lovers learn to play themselves.

Body shape is irrelevant to the Magician. The Magician connects to the soul, not the form. Magicians are free from visual prejudice. Likewise with gender roles. Many of the Magicians we have met in our professional work don't care whether they are with males or females. Although they may have a personal preference for one gender or the other, it's irrelevant to the work they do.

Author Anne Rice has been asked how she is able to portray sex between two men so passionately and accurately. She replies that when the energy gets intense enough it no longer has all those little divisions. It's like molten metal.

As the Quakers say, "You are but a clay vessel. May the light of God shine through you." In the Magician, you give away your body to the higher good. And you are rewarded with a deep "Knowing" of where to guide the sexual charge of the moment.

Meaning and Mastery

Meaning is not given to you on a silver platter. You *create* meaning in the Magician. You teach yourself to be a master of your fate, to choreograph your life, to live with *intention*. Here in the Magician you *co-create* with the gods. You know your strengths and your limits. You are a master of aligning yourself with your and your partner's *natural* sexual energy. You make things look easier than they are, because, as in Aikido, you roll with the natural forces. In accepting your innate nature, you truly live out the aphorism, "The universe knows no no's."

THE JOURNEY OF THE SEXUAL ARCHETYPES: HEALING AND TEACHING SEXUALITY

The Magician is an important "gateway of initiation," where you move from self to other, from just the two of you to the whole tribe, the whole society. Thereby, you heartily choose to serve the group vision, to serve others—even from within the intimate privacy of your bedroom.

In the Magician, you transition from the personal to the collective. You are prepared to give freely, to be an instrument for the healing of others. This archetype is a teacher, a healer, a temple priestess, a sexual shaman, a tantric initiator, a loving mentor. You are choreographers of the sexual dance, the sexual magician, even the sex therapist, or the sexual surrogate, maybe even the "sacred prostitute." You are connected to both the magic and the mundane. As the Magician, you mirror the beauty of the soul and the power of love to your partner.

An uplifting example of the Magician is *Don Quixote de La Mancha,* Cervantes's classic Spanish novel, popularized in the play and movie, *Man of La Mancha.* In one scene, Don Quixote comes upon a destitute scrub maid. But Don Quixote sees only beauty and grace. Rather than being stuck on the "reality" of poor Aldonza, Don Quixote worships her as Dulcinea, "a sweet lady and a fair virgin." *Man of La Mancha* is a kind of passion play, and indeed Aldonza resurrects herself as Dulcinea. She is transformed. The Magician is alive and well in this play.

For a powerful direct portrayal of the Magician sexual archetype head on, do not miss the Canadian film *Bliss.* This remarkable film courageously gives an insiders' intimate, gentle look at the hidden and valuable profession of sexual surrogacy. In *Wild Orchid,* Mickey Rourke's cynicism and hurt are burned by the love and presence of the one he loves. Veronica Franco, the Italian courtesan in *Dangerous Beauty,* is a healer to many.

One of the clearest contemporary examples of the Magician can be found in the 1991 film *Prince of Tides*. In this film, both Nick Nolte's and Barbra Streisand's characters are suffering from debilitating wounds: his, a sexual one; hers, an emotional one. Each plays the Magician for the other—though not simultaneously—so that both can overcome their hurts and get on with their lives.

The Magician archetype is a healer or mentor: He or she is deeply concerned with helping the lover overcome a hurdle, recover from a wound, or achieve a new level of mastery. In addition to the body and mind, the Magician provides a connection with the spirit.

The Sexual Fire

The Magician has mastered the fire: The healer knows how to coax it higher or lower, as needed. Master Magicians have trained themselves in the techniques of delayed orgasm, controlling their chakras and the movement of energy within their bodies. Many have become adept at Taoist and tantric approaches.

The Magician is a seasoned archetype, a voice of experience. He or she understands the aging process. When we all age, we're faced with the task of letting go of our bodies as we get closer to death. The Magician looks beyond the frail, temporal bag of flesh and into the ageless, unkillable soul.

We have encountered many people in our clinical practices who say, "I don't like his body any more. He's gained twenty pounds." To the Magician, such a thing is irrelevant. The Magician says, "I love you because I see your soul." The Magician's acceptance of their lovers runs very deep.

Sex performer and educator Annie Sprinkle is a prime example of a sexual Magician and healer. During her stage shows she holds up photographs of people she's had sex with. The audience is always struck by the diversity of her partners' physical forms: Some are obese, some are wheelchair-bound, others have obvious physical challenges. Her lovers' physical form is irrelevant. She has moved beyond mere bodily shapes and physical appearance. She makes love to the soul within each of them.

Though common in many other cultures, the Magician archetype has largely disappeared from contemporary American culture or rather its expression is unacknowledged. Sexual wounding is not uncommon and many relationships are called to be a healing ground, the place where we unzip our most sensitive places. The conscious presence of the Magician in the bedroom and the permission to make space for what needs to be healed is vital to reconnect sexual pleasure and personal power.

In the Magician, we begin to give back to our partner the wisdom and skills we've gained. The Magician holds a place of knowledge, and is a safe container and an access to what is larger than your personal story, to what is truly healing.

The Magician's concentration is split: While he or she is constantly tracking his or her own feelings, he or she is deeply focused on what is happening to his or her partner. The Magician's skill is sophisticated; he or she knows how to use sexual energy the way a magician knows how to use cosmic energy. The Magician is perhaps the least familiar archetype in contemporary American culture. We have little knowledge of the sacred prostitutes and temple priestesses of certain other cultures.

How to Get Started

The best way to experience the Magician archetype is to create and perform a "Healing Ceremony." One of you will take on the role of the Magician, the other can even be in another archetype.

If, for example, the ceremony you choose to create is a Rite of Initiation, your partner could be in the role of the Innocent, as the neophyte or initiate.

As with each archetype, the first step is to talk it out with your partner. Tell each other about times you were wounded, sexually or emotionally. For many people, the origin of this wound goes all the way back to their very first sexual experience. Talk about the areas in which you feel sexually blocked, inhibited, or where you feel growth is needed. Together, find out for each of you what needs to be healed or what needs to be expanded. Listen nonjudgmentally, with the whole of your being.

Next, discuss the type of ceremony you'd like to have. Depending upon your objective, you could choose to perform any of the following:

An Initiation Ceremony: This is a good choice if some new experience is a first time for one of you, or if another first time was horrible, and you wish to reinvent it. A ceremony of initiation can be a beautiful, meaningful way to welcome a lover into sexuality, or to bring the lover over the threshold into a new sexual realm.

An Apprenticeship Ceremony: If one of you is older and/or more experienced, and will be introducing the other to many new sexual realms and techniques, you may wish to conduct a ceremony in which you formally meet each other as Teacher and Student. The purpose of this ceremony is to establish the roles and their dynamics. We have occasionally recommended this type of ceremony in our clinical practice for couples who feel inhibited because one of them is more experienced than the other. Allowing the less experienced partner to perform in the role of the Teacher can imbue that partner with confidence, and helps to balance the relationship.

A Confrontation Ceremony: In this type of ceremony, one of you will actively confront and work through some aspect of sexuality which makes you feel afraid or uncomfortable. We recommend caution here: This ceremony is for couples who have established a great deal of trust and connection, and must only be performed if the partner who is to confront their fear is ready and willing. In this ceremony, the partner who is in the role of Magician acts as shepherd and coach, supporting the lover through the area of difficulty.

A Teaching Ceremony: Often one partner will be motivated to learn a new sexual technique, and will wish to teach it to the other. You may choose to study tantric technique or Taoist teaching. Or you may wish to learn specific techniques such as erotic massage, breath work, G-spot work, or you might simply go through a classic sexuality book such as the *Kama Sutra* or *The Art of Sexual Ecstasy*. Then you can create a ceremony in which you pass your new knowledge on to your partner.

Your Own Designer Ceremony: Talk together about the time, place, tone, and other particulars of your ritual. Many people like to get out into nature for this type of experience. For some, the gist of the ceremony is simply to allow themselves to be touched lovingly, for a long period of time, without feeling like they need to do anything in order to be loved. Many women find this to be a powerful experience, because they've come to believe that they have to "give sex" in order to get love. Simply being loved deeply without having to "put out" can be a tremendously opening experience for them. Your ceremony can be a one-time event or a series of ritual encounters.

As the Magician, you're the one who is orchestrating the invention of the ceremony. You're creating it together, of course, but the Magician is the one who asks the questions, who keeps the investigation moving and the creativity flowing.

The Magician is also the one who prepares the ceremony. Begin the preparations about a week in advance. As the Magician, you will place the candles, provide the music, pour the water for washing feet, and so forth. Ritual space must be sacred; make it so by preparing it with great care and minute attention to details. As the week goes by you will receive more clarity about what needs to be done.

It is part of the Magician's role to open yourself to the unknown, to receive the information coming in the form of intuition, dreams, a book passing your desk, a conversation with a friend. It's your job to trust the unknown.

As the week progresses, check in with the initiate from time to time. The connection between you is a vital element of the ceremony. You might also give the initiate some preparatory task, such as writing down her feelings about the upcoming initiation, or writing about how she prevents herself from experiencing full pleasure. The one other task that belongs to the initiate during this stage is to find or make a gift to bring to the Magician to thank him for the wisdom he is about to impart.

On the day of the ceremony, while the initiate is getting ready, prepare the space, light some candles, and invite the spirit to be with you. Say a prayer, or do whatever is meaningful in your tradition to ask the Healing entities to be present. Just before you begin, talk to each other about how you feel. Spend some time looking at each other. Breathe together, your mouths next to each other. Connect your hearts with your genitals. Acknowledge your love for each other.

Now, let the ceremony begin. As the Magician, come with a plan in mind, but be open to change at any moment. If something is not working, let it go. If you feel disconnected, stop what you are doing and find out how you can connect.

At the end of your ceremony, sit facing each other. Say whatever needs to be said. Then blow out the candles, give thanks to the spirit, and close the ceremony. This ritual closing of the ceremony is extremely important, because it signals the end of your time in these roles. When all is finished, nestle in one another's arms. In the days that follow, make time to check in with each other, and to talk about the experience.

Costumes and Props

The Magician, also called the Healer, is the one who takes care of all the food, music, and other miscellaneous details. The Healer runs the show. Dress for the role of the Healer in whatever calls to mind images of benign power: the robe of a magician or priest, for example. The partner who is to be healed may wish to dress in the ritual white of the initiate.

Casting the Stars

In the archetypes we've discussed previously, the primary focus was on the individual's own pleasure and responses. In this archetype, the Magician's circle of concern goes from "me" to "us." But even though Healers are deeply focused on their lovers, they never lose their awareness of what's going on within themselves. This is what allows them to enter into a deeply empathetic awareness of their partner: Every change, every nuance their lover experiences resonates within their own being. The Magician is intensely aware of shifts in the lover's demeanor. He or she knows at once when something new has happened. The Magician is the shepherd of the lover's epiphanies.

The Magician takes on the role of attentive mentor or loving choreographer, to help the lover overcome a difficult obstacle, a phase of growth, or an emotional hurt. The Magician understands that a wound has left the lover afraid to reach beyond the "safe" place. The Magician takes partners by the hand and helps them take a risk that they might not be able to handle alone. The Magician also provides a witness to the partner's wounding. The simple act of witnessing the hurt can facilitate healing.

The Magician's relationship to the lover, like that of a teacher to a student, is one of unequal power. If one partner is always in the position of Magician, it's difficult to maintain a relationship of equals.

Many times, not one but both partners are suffering from wounds. They may try to get close, but something keeps triggering their pain, and they move away. This is a dynamic that can be changed through the archetype of the Magician. Each member of the couple can take a turn in the role of Magician. Simply having one of the pair play the Healer for the other is often enough to open them up. Later, they'll switch roles. When wounds are no longer the issue in a relationship, lovers can use the Healer archetype to propel each other to ever greater creative heights.

The Shadow

The Shadow side of the Magician is particularly ominous: You may be tempted to use the Magician's power for your own agenda. There are numerous sex scandals involving spiritual teachers misusing their power for sexual favors, which illustrate the extreme case of this Shadow.

The Shadow of the Magician is the inability to see your lovers as being greater than they see themselves. If you can't do this, you aren't capable of shepherding their growth. As Antoine de Saint-Exupéry says, "What is essential is invisible to the eye."

("L'essentiel est invisible pour les yeux.") When we fail to see that which is invisible, we've succumbed to the Shadow. This is the tyranny of the ordinary world of information, of the prosaic and the normal. This is the disease of lack of meaning and absence of passion.

The Shadow of the Magician also emerges when someone who is supposed to hold the container doesn't. The difference in power between the Magician and the lover is supposed to be a benign difference. But the dark temptation of the Magician is to misuse that power difference for his or her own ends. We see this all the time in cinema depictions of religious leaders who molest their followers, and in the newspapers, in various stories of doctors who get sexual with their patients.

Magicians also face the Shadow in the form of their own limitations and the lack of healing of their own wounds. Magicians are unable to heal in any area where they're judgmental, or where their own wounds are triggered. Avoid the Shadow by carefully checking your motivations. You must be giving freely, without judgment, expecting nothing in return.

LESSONS

When one partner is struggling to overcome a sexual or emotional hurt, planning and carrying out a Healing ceremony can be a tremendous source of comfort, strength, and renewal. During the ceremony, the wounded person may allow the Magician to lovingly caress the area where they were wounded for hours at a time.

The greatest joy of the Magician is to restore the sparkle to their lover's eyes, to see their sexual "burner" turned up a notch, to see the magic return to their soul. This is reward enough for them. Magicians get turned on just by watching people open up, by seeing the epiphany in their eyes. Their joy is to expand the sexual universe of someone else. They receive a pleasure that is deeply erotic, almost voyeuristic, from watching their lovers vault obstacles. In much the same way that teaching feeds the teacher, healing provides the Magician with exhilaration.

The Magician sees how people are real, palpable beings, just like them. Magicians understand that everything that goes around comes around. They know that when you do something to hurt your partner it comes back to you.

Magicians also enjoy the peaceful satisfaction of resolved conflict. This doesn't mean that they have no more conflict, only that they are at peace with the paradox within them. Like Buddha, the Magician hasn't vanquished the demon, but instead has invited it to tea. The Healer lives out the advice from the Bible's Book of Hebrews: "Be not afraid to entertain strangers, for thereby some have entertained angels unawares."

Magicians work their restorative magic through their own experience of deep connection. When all is said and done, it's the lack of connection that is behind every wound that has been inflicted upon us. Magicians experience this connection as a palpable thing. They see the common bond between all individuals, as well as the link between an individual's body and soul. It is from this profound experience of connection that Magicians gather their power. Magicians help restore their lovers' connection to others, which may have been severed by an emotional wound. Magicians are able to help their lovers reconnect to their bodies by providing the ingredients and the space for healing to take place.

YOUR TURN

Here are some ideas to get started in the Magician archetype:

- Create a healing ceremony for something you're afraid of

- Try teaching a new sexual technique
- Discuss who has the most power in your relationship; then have the other partner embody the Magician for an evening
- Try learning about G-spot massage, or prostate and anal massage
- Celebrate being a slut, imagine what that could mean

Onward

Now you have arrived at a place of knowledge with the ability to connect profoundly. The lessons of being present to yourself and to others have grounded you. You are now ready to enter the presence of the Divine, of pure connection with others.

CHAPTER EIGHT

Merging with the Fire

THE MYSTIC

"As the river gives itself to the ocean,
what is inside me moves inside you."

Kabir, 15th-century poet

We jogged to Oona's this time. But it felt more like flying, as if carried on the wings of angels. Oona said that was the feeling of being in the "Zone." Welcome to the Mystic sexual archetype! Time to let go. Time to merge with the universe, time for cosmic sex.

People think they have to "get out of" their bodies in order to hang out with the deities. In the Mystic, our assignment is to use our physical—even sweaty—bodies as our spaceship, to blast off and soar in the star-filled, far reaches of the heavens.

I couldn't wait to jog home, get out of my clothes and get into the Zone with Michael.

— Michelle

Luckily Michael and Michelle have experienced the "Zone" before, in athletics and music. We will see shortly how they find the Zone in their lovemaking.

But first, have you made love to the whole universe at once? Have you ever gotten so intoxicated with the flood of sexual energy that you forgot you were you? Have you lost track of where your body ended and your partner's body began? Have you had a religious experience during sex? Have you ever practiced tantric sex? Have you felt merged with the all-knowing, all-present white-light Creator of the universe during sex? Have you lost track of time and space?

If so, then you may know the ways of the Mystic. If not, then come with us on an enchanted voyage of the Starship Intercourse. Leave all your earthly possessions behind, including yourself. Oh, but don't forget your sacred body! Don't leave it behind. Your body is the latest-model spaceship, the best ever designed. Pleasure will be your fuel, enchantment your star map, bright eyes your porthole to vast intergalactic regions.

Here's a quick look at the sexual electricity of the Mystic:

- Like entering an altered state, being inebriated
- Pleasure feels light and pure, open and plentiful, a gift of the gods
- Heavenly, divine, soaring with the deities, spiritual
- Pure, undifferentiated life-force energy
- There is no self, no other, no partner, no bedroom, no distinct "things"
- Dionysian, feasting, whole-bodied, physical, and spiritual
- No holding back, not cautious, unthinking, uninhibited

When you're "inside" the Mystic archetype, you desire:

- To be transported to the never-never land of pure bliss

- Spirit, transcendence, revitalization
- The feeling that the whole universe is made out of endless pleasure
- To merge with your partner, you, and the universe—to have no boundaries
- Not to need to care about your partner, or anyone, or anything—all is well
- To leave your ego at your therapist's office, your worries back on planet Earth
- To let go, to be light, to have expansive all-encompassing passion for pure life
- To have a religious experience in bed with your partner
- To dive into an "altered state" of consciousness
- To soar on the wings of angels, to glide through star-filled, bliss-filled galaxies

When we describe the Mystic archetype to people, we usually get one of two wildly different reactions. Either the Mystic seems quite familiar, or it is as alien as a flying saucer landing in their backyard.

For some people, the Mystic is as familiar as drinking a glass of water. The ability to enter the realm of the sacred is easily accessible as the outside life and the inner life are intimately connected with each other. Making love is a reconnection with the Mystery.

For other people, the Mystic is so alien, when we describe this archetype to them, all we get is a puzzled, "Huh?" with a scrunched-up expression wrinkling across their faces. If you are a "huh?" person, don't worry. If your first reaction to the Mystic is an instant, "I just don't get it, what on earth are you talking about?" it's quite okay.

Many people need to be "grounded" in reality. When they travel from "here" to "there," they like to know all the intermediate stepping stones in between. These people feel naked without their GPS, or their AAA maps. Their approach to life has its own charms. This is the classic "engineer" who wants to concentrate on "just the facts, ma'am."

For the Mystic you might think that heavenly "artists" would have an advantage over the earthbound "engineers." But remember what Oona told Michelle and Michael about not abandoning their bodies, about going *through* their bodies to the heavens.

> *Oona said people think they have to "get out of" their bodies in order to hang out with the deities. In the Mystic, our assignment is to use our physical—even sweaty—bodies as our spaceship, to blast off and soar in the star-filled, far reaches of the heavens.*
>
> — Michelle

Many Mystics try to take a shortcut to heaven, skipping over the physical realm. They have to remember to bring their sensuous, pleasure-yearning bodies *with* them on their poetic voyages. To descend into the body; to learn to spin straw into gold; to turn prosaic physicality into poetic star travel.

Almost everyone has some place in their life where they have encountered the Mystic, sometime, somewhere. The key is to find that place and *begin* there.

SEX AT THE "TOP OF THE MOUNTAIN"

To give you more of a "feel" for the Mystic, let's return to our South Seas paradise the *Island of Yes* and see where you might encounter the Mystic there. It's probably best just to buy a plane ticket and go there right now. Short of that, *imagine* you're there.

It's daybreak. You have spent the night at the Tribal Dance of the Magician, finally curling up together around the fire, sleeping soundly snuggled together.

You open your eyes to the gray-blue sky of the early morning, hints of pink on the few wispy clouds on the horizon, mostly hidden by the rain forest. Tropical songbirds are awakening, too, chirping in a brand new good morning and calling you to arise.

In perfect, reverent silence, you hold hands and head up a well-cared-for trail into the jungle, twisting up the side of the central mountain of the Island. Up you go, walking faster now, hardly noticing each other, just feeling your bare feet padding against the soft volcanic black soil, your bare skin growing moist and slick, sweat beading up your chest, muscles pushing you up higher now. The curve of the seashore is now visible.

The trail flattens now as you wind past the last few curves to the peak. At the top, you nestle together, speechless, as you gaze out at the circular sweep of the entire Island of Yes. A warm sea breeze towels your skin dry and caresses the tender grasses under you as you lie down in the rose glow of the dawn.

The sun peeks above the distant edge of the world. White sunlight blasts through your bodies, already moving in rhythm to the waves of sultry wind coming in from high over the Pacific. You make love at the Top of the Mountain in ecstatic union, merged with sea and air, earth and fire, you and the infinite divine.

Sex in the Mystic

Let's join Michelle and Michael now to see how they merge with their Creator.

Michelle says I've changed. I think she might be right. I was such a meat and potatoes guy just a few months ago—at least when it came to sex.

If Oona had told me about the Mystic when we first starting going to her, I would have thought she was ready for the loony bin. I mean, how could a roll in the hay have anything to do with interstellar cosmic travel, or communing with the gods?

But when Michelle and I were jogging earlier today, I got into the Zone, too. I'd never really thought about it before. I just did it. Now I was getting more conscious of this "otherworldly" feeling that I have lots of times—in the shower, in that half-awake netherworld when I'm just waking up in the morning, or that time when Michelle and I climbed Mt. Whitney and we were looking out from on top of the world.

So when we got home that evening, I noticed Michelle's eyes were glowing, just like they had when we'd been jogging.

She lit some candles, and I noticed I was paying more attention to the candles than to Michelle slipping off her running shorts, and unlatching her bra. I shed my clothes, still mesmerized by the flickering of the candles.

My memory blurs a little at this point. I remember sliding naked in between the smooth, clean sheets, and hugging each other in full toe-to-head-to-toe embrace. It seemed like every inch of our skin was touching, merging, becoming the same body. Our bodies moved together as if they were in charge of the evening—not us. And we seemed to know to get out of the way.

It really was a lot like the Zone that I get into listening to music or playing tennis. It wasn't some weird mystical experience that only gurus in India could do. But I'm not giving myself enough credit here. Making love with Michelle that night was about as mystical as any place any guru has ever been. I'm sure of that.

As our sexual tempo quickened, Michelle's pelvis got into a gentle yet powerful rocking back-and-forth rhythm.

Our genitals merged. They just joined into one ball of fire on their own without missing a wave of those underwater undulations. On we went, paradoxically in our own ecstatic worlds, and yet fused seamlessly, forever, eternally together.

I was inside Michelle. She was inside me. We made love to the universe that night.

— Michael

Sex in the Mystic is a departure from "normal" sex—not just a departure from planet Earth. If you are like many people, you were probably raised to think sex is about connecting with your sweetie, about paying attention, and becoming ever more intimate with your partner.

And yet shockingly enough, the Mystic calls you to almost *ignore* your partner and to pay attention to something else instead: the whole universe. Sometimes in the Mystic you may feel like there's only you, other times there's only the all-encompassing spirit world. Either way, your partner is not your focus per se as you are one, not separated. Ironically, this mind-altered, being-altered voyage can bring you closer to your partner than ever before!

At its best, you return from sex in the Mystic having traveled to the same supernovas and distant frontiers of the galaxy as your partner. You may have met the transcendent, the spark, the sparkle, the life-force itself—and met each other in a new way. And you can bring the "force" back to planet Earth and into your relationship. Your relationship will be renewed, revitalized, and re-energized as never before.

If this description of the Mystic reminds you of Beatles songs of gurus in India cajoling us to lose our minds, you're getting it. There is a sexual practice inspired by Eastern religions called tantra which combines prayerful meditation with full-on sex. That combination might seem incongruous at first, but it is very powerful and as respectful as any spiritual practice. Indeed, the Mystic can be thought of as a spiritual practice, a form of prayer drawing us closer to the eternal heartbeat of Creation.

The Mystic at its best is vital to keeping relationships bright-eyed and magical. But, as you can imagine, any archetype which calls you to "ignore" your partner has its pitfalls and red-flag cautions. We will talk more later about the Shadow of the Mystic, and what to watch out for.

For the moment, we suggest you just dive into the Mystic and "get out of the way." Here are a few tips to get you started. Sex in the Mystic is:

- Spiritual, otherworldly, awe-inspiring, transcendent, prayerful, soulful, mystical
- Full-bodied, physical, immediate, present
- Ignoring your physical body, while using and enjoying your physical body
- Paradoxical, both-and, you and not-you, heaven and earth
- Body and spirit, mindless and mindful, here and not here
- In the Zone, tantric, the "Buddhism" or "Zen" of sex
- Unfettered, unbound, unleashed
- Timeless, eternal, once-upon-a-time, poetic
- Cosmic, grand, magnificent, intergalactic
- Caring, touching, eye-to-eye; embodiment of total love

As with other sexual archetypes, don't hold back. Try it. Fake it till you make it. Here are a few don'ts and dos to help you navigate on your interplanetary voyage:

- *Don't* joke, but don't be too serious, either.

- *Don't* worry about the day-to-day logistics, traffic, grocery lists.
- *Don't* "sweat the small stuff," don't get hung up on details.
- *Don't* hold on to anything, don't hold back, don't limit yourself.
- *Don't* chatter, don't comment, don't think too much, don't talk.
- *Don't* come right away, don't get on the "freight train" toward orgasm.
- *Don't* forget that you are alive and have a body—now.!

- *Do* prepare your space, light candles, turn off the phone, take a tantra class.
- *Do* let yourself be ecstatic, feel your skin, know that you are alive.
- *Do* be in an altered state, drunk on life, inebriated on magic and miracles.
- *Do* breathe, feel the rhythm, hear the pulse of your body and the universe as one.
- *Do* delay coming, delay ejaculating.
- *Do* follow the energy, get out of the way.
- *Do* stay in eye-to-eye soul connection, look as Athena does beyond the horizon.
- *Do* look *through* your partner, not *at* him or her.
- *Do* make contact with the life force itself, pure spirit, pure energy, pure divine.
- *Do* let your imagination soar, feel that anything is possible, think lovely thoughts.
- *Do* sing praises to the Universe, to Creation, to the All-Loving Master of the Universe.
- *Do* adore, touch, caress, make beautiful, soulful love with your cherished partner.

There is a saying that if God wanted to hide somewhere where no one would ever think to look, God would hide within each of us. We'd have to look into each other's eyes to find God. This saying captures the essence of the Mystic.

Your Arousal

In the Mystic you are aroused by beauty itself—the beauty of sitting on a mountain peak, the beauty of looking deeply into your partner's eyes, or the beauty of just being alive and breathing sweet, life-giving air through our nostrils. To get in the mood, you might find a place in nature which inspires you. Or you might read poetry together. Or just sit facing each other on the living room floor. Oftentimes it is the Mystic who calls us to make plane reservations to fly to a Caribbean beach for that dream vacation. Go ahead. You can read this book on the plane.

Sexuality for this archetype is a Mystic union. There is no self-involvement, no other person there when this intercourse of self and other becomes a Mystic Union. The poetry of Rumi and Hafiz speaks of this state where the beloved may be flesh or not. It is a tantric path, the path of spirit. There is no difference between other and me, body and soul, desire and spirit, hunger and satisfaction. I *am* and I am surrendered. You freely move from the form to the formless, from the asexual to the erotic.

The purpose of sexual encounters in the Mystic is to raise energy for ecstatic experience. The Mystic lover knows how to raise, channel, move, and hold energy, so that pure essence is felt by both of you. Essence includes self and lover, stillness and movement. The Mystic makes love with the whole universe.

Your Relationship with Your Body

The Mystic's sexuality is rooted in the experience that your body, mind, and spirit are one. That body, sex, and the sacred are one. To the Mystic, sexuality is a practice or an experience to connect with spirit. In that experience, you are not attached to the form. It is the soul that moves you. The sexuality of the Mystic is timeless, magical, connected, and transcendent. The connection is experienced at every moment. Your whole body is involved in the dance, from your little toe to the top of your head.

As a Mystic lover you have the ability to contain your own energy without dispersing it, building up an intense charge, moving the energy like waves in the ocean.

The skill of moving energy requires your body to be a strong container and at the same time an open channel. You surrender yourself and love the wave, the rhythm of the universe pulses through your body, you become one with the ebb and flow of the ocean. You are the ocean. You are deeply attuned to your body. All those components are present in the experience. The Mystic is a place where you are both *within* the experience and a witness to it at the same time.

Traveling through space and time and the shape-shifting forms of the body are frequent experiences of the Mystic. Some have been known to visit the ancient pyramids of Egypt, and make love on the banks of the Nile; others have swum in the deep depths of the ocean—all from the coziness of their suburban bedrooms.

Flirting

Flirting for the Mystic is present and real. It is not a play. It is Eros being experienced whether we are aroused or not. Eros the creative energy is always around and present. One of our best flirting memories involved a Buddhist monk because he was so present to the aliveness of pure connection.

Your Emotions

Many of us have experienced this archetype within our lifetimes; several of our clients wistfully describe the magic spell that once wove itself about their bedroom, and express a longing to return to it, or a sorrow that they cannot journey there with their current partners. One client told us, "Thank you for naming it."

When we are in the Mystic archetype, emotions are elated. They move freely, you can cry and laugh and pass through every emotion. You are not attached to any of them. One moment, tears pass and the next, a smile. Every emotion is exposed, one after the other. We become an open book, a reflection of the wealth of being human. You see your lover's face ever changing right before your eyes and you get to be there with them and there is a sense of abandonment you share close up.

The characteristic of the Mystic is that what is felt is so unnamable and indefinable that it can only pass through you. If you try to hold on to any of the emotions—poof, they're gone. The space you enter into is also so large. The Mystic flows with emotion and has the ability to sustain being open. It is actually a requirement to sustain openness regardless of what shows up.

The Mystic has the ability to stay in the middle of this emotional fire. It is a place where relationship touches the mystical and binds us beyond the struggle of personalities.

When a relationship touches the Mystic easily, it does not imply that you will necessarily live day to day easily. Some people do heaven well together. Some people do hell well together. The ability to navigate your day-to-day life is held by other archetypes. Relationships where the magic is strong and the daily living is challenging can be difficult, because of the deep karmic connection that exists.

Your Erotic Fire

In the Mystic, your erotic fire is the same fire which lights the stars, the same fire which inflames your partner's irrepressible passion for you. In the Mystic, when you join your genitals with your partner's, the eternal feminine and masculine are being joined at that very same exquisite moment. All of Creation is singing out at the wonder of this sacred, jubilant moment of continuing birthing of the universe.

Words are inadequate to describe the brilliance of the erotic fire of the Mystic. We can only demonstrate our devotion to the fire by diving into it, surrendering to it, and merging totally with it, and with all vibrating, pulsing universal matter.

Your Orgasms and Sexual Ceremony

Time to return to Michelle and Michael to hear how the Mystic bestowed them with a profound experience.

I'm still vibrating from Michael's and my orgasmic bliss, but I never would have expected how it happened, and why it was so off the charts. It was our "sexual ceremony." It sounds kind of strange to combine something that sounds religious with sex. But we tried it anyway. Now I am a total convert. .

Dr. Oona told us that orgasm is always—but especially in the Mystic—a place where we can actually change who we are, change our life patterns. It's as if we're computers, and at the moment of orgasm, we get to hit the "reset button." We can "re-program" who we are in that golden moment. That's if we're prepared and conscious of the new people we want to become.

I'm not usually very conscious during orgasm, so I wasn't sure this was going to work too well. Oona said that the important thing is preparing ahead of time, taking some quiet time either alone or with Michael to declare our intensions. Michael said he wanted to figure out what his "home" sexual archetype is. I wanted to get closer to Michael in our relationship.

We took these "intentions" and turned them into shorthand "images." Michael's image was a house with us making love on the roof. I thought that was funny. But it worked for him. My image was picturing us facing each other, naked, holding hands, sitting in each other's laps. I was sure I could remember my image no matter how hot we got together.

So there we were with candles casting their flickering yellow glow in our sacred love temple. Michael moved slowly inside me, each sway of his hips exploding through me. Except it wasn't Michael. It wasn't even a person. It was pure golden silken strands of heaven itself, massaging the inner walls of a cathedral as big as the sky. Spiraling fireballs were arcing out of my vagina, from the center vortex of the galaxy, into my whole being, into all that I know, all that I have ever known.

Occasionally, that image of Michael and me sitting in each other's naked laps would wash through my shimmering consciousness. And then vanish. And starlight would again illuminate the inner core of my being as bright as the moon.

Waves of bliss cascaded through my body, as if all of me was just pure fire, pure radiant energy, leaving a sense of the closeness I so desire with Michael.

After that blowout orgasm, I think we fell asleep. But in a way, that orgasm is still buzzing inside me. That intention I brought into our sexual ceremony, as Oona calls it, is with me every day now—guiding me ever closer to my beloved.

— Michelle

In the Mystic, orgasms are crossroads, places where you can change life directions. In a traffic circle, you can come in on one spoke, and leave on a different spoke. Orgasms are similar. In the Mystic you can leave orgasm on a different life "spoke." You get to focus your "intention" to guide your life energy in a new direction. You can take this intention into orgasm. Here in the *void* of orgasm, all is *possible,* including the new directions you wish for yourself. You have the opportunity to be changed, be transformed.

The key to this remarkable power of the Mystic is *preparation.* In order to "harness" the power of the Mystic's orgasm, you must be clear about this new direction you are wanting for yourself. Furthermore, you must translate all the feelings and words which make up this intention, into a single compact "image" or symbol. It is this "icon" which represents the entirety of the intention. "Pack lightly" for orgasm. Take only the minimum. Just take the icon. That's all you need. Hold this in your mind, in your body, in your spirit while you begin to make love.

And don't worry. If you are prepared, the icon will come with you to just before orgasm. What happens at orgasm itself is not your concern. Just enjoy your orgasm. And if somehow you forget everything and drop the icon back in foreplay, it's OK, too. You can always have another juicy sexual ceremony another time. The deities are gracious and generous. Just remember to thank them.

Also, orgasms in the Mystic are full bodied. There is so much energy to discharge—the energy of the whole universe—that the genitals are not big enough. Let the orgasmic energy flood your whole body and beyond. Let the energy explode out the top of your head, out the "crown chakra." Try not to go quickly into a "final" orgasm like ejaculation for men. The Mystic is multiply orgasmic for both men and women.

The Journey of the Sexual Archetypes: Spiritual Sexuality

The task is the integration of the spirit. We are ready to experience heaven and the union with the Divine, to sit with the God and Goddess, we are the ancient stag and the priestess who mate ceremonially at Beltane. This is the blessed union joining the earthly, earthy stag with the heavenly, sacred deities. There is no self-involvement and no "other" when this intercourse of self and lover becomes a mystic union.

The poetry of Rumi and Hafiz speaks of this state, as do Annie Sprinkle's rites of passion, and the merging of Mickey Rourke and Jacqueline Bisset at the end of *Wild Orchid*.

The Mystic experiences sex as a prayer, a tantric dance where time and space disappear, where we are the river of love itself, the loved and the beloved.

The Mystic is a place of heaven of merging with the divine. After our discovering the many landscapes of our erotic nature, we meet with the Beloved and soar to heaven. The Mystic lives in an altered dimension, in the magical space of the deities. It is spirit, it is power and surrender as one, it is union beyond forms, the space beyond gender and personality. Soul meeting soul, spirit meeting spirit in the universal dance that existed forever.

Up to this point of the journey, the fire was separate from us, even if it surrounded and permeated us, and gave us a wonderful life-animating and life-transforming heat and light. But the fire was a gift from "out there," a place of separation where however subtle still there remains a sense of you and me as separate entity. In the Mystic, perfectly aligned with the fire, we are also aligned with its source: spirit. In the Sensualist, the fire was kindled in our loins, our genitals, and our skin; for the erotic Mystic, the fire burns according to its own design in every cell of our body, in every tingle of our spine, in every fiery breath. Only in this single eternal breath and heartbeat, the potential for the Mystic is to erotically merge with the whole universe, making love with the fire which lights up the whole world.

In the Mystic, we offer our self to spirit, our soul, our body. We are once again with the Creation beyond any duality. It is an experience beyond prayer, where prayers are answered and where we are in a state of grace. The other, the Beloved, larger than the self is a gateway.

Mystics are the Stag and the Priestess meeting to fertilize the field at Beltane, the archetypal world meeting the archetypal world. In the Mystic, we are carried by something beyond our understanding, connected to the matrix of life, to life as a whole. The energy streaming through our body is Creation itself. We make love with the sky, the moon, the stars, and all that Creation contains. It is a state of timelessness, of expansion with the whole world as a playground. It is a grand fireworks of our sexuality. The Mystic is a walk into multiple realities where we transcend time, space, and matter. Connected to our true essence, we are fully available to the experience, fully present to each moment and our bodies are immersed in the fire, transformed by the fire, one with the fire.

The task of the Mystic is the integration of the spirit beyond the material, to open the world of sexuality to what is beyond the sexual. Through the eyes of the Mystic, our Beloved is beautiful regardless of form. The hag is transformed into the Beloved, we see beauty in its pure existence.

The Mystic is an unmated archetype in the sense of being partnered or married to a person. The Mystic is rather mated to the whole of creation. The Mystic archetype is where you connect with your partner soul to soul, where you recognize each other as soul mates in this moment in time, as part of the same mind. This is the archetype that will cement the connection, give it some depth, and make clear the karmic connection in this very moment. The personality has been washed away and what is left is the pure essence. In that place, only love exists.

The Mystic is the ideal archetype to expand our understanding of the world and reality, to see with a different vision and to get familiar with the realm of spirit. Regular visits to the mystical realm will anchor our knowledge that what we see of the world is just a small part of the whole.

In the Mystic, we become gods and goddesses themselves, not just their reflection. What is required of us is to surrender the personal and the self to what is larger than ourselves.

For some of us, the Mystic seems far out, too "new-agey," too "woo-woo" and inaccessible. But mystical experiences are very real to those who have them. One day, we don't know why, but there is this magic. It just happens. Suddenly, we are in a different dimension where the time has stopped. Knowing the way to go back there requires skill, presence, and grace. We can prepare all the ingredients to make an outstanding culinary delight, but the true magic itself enters on its own.

Costumes and Props

The Mystic archetype lives in the realm of "ceremonial" space. Indeed, Michael and Michelle decided to set up a magical space for their encounter. They brought in the candles, incense, and chose a costume that conveyed timeless magic. They became timeless figures. They chose a music that brought them to a different landscape. Their music was perhaps ethereal, for example, Indian music, transporting them through the ages.

The Mystic archetype is a prayer for the spirit and sometimes out of nowhere, we find ourselves in this place of magic. It often happens like that, an unexpectedly and out-of-nowhere opening through the door. But certain practices will help to provide us access through this doorway. However, the access is always a gift. In many ways, it is like the experience of meditation. Sometimes, in beginner's luck, we touch the Buddha's mind. We touch our Buddha nature until the mind kicks in and we wonder what happened. Or we might feel special or want to reproduce the experience and bang, it's gone. Spiritual sex is a little bit like that, except that the body experience helps to stay in contact with the Buddha nature. You can go in this ecstatic state of meditation much longer, being led by the body and not by the mind. Practices such as tantra, Taoist yoga, or other forms of yoga open the body to accessing these ecstatic states.

Setting the Space

For the Mystic, the whole world is the "container" or the space. The experience is one of expansion, of traveling to the edges of the universe. What makes this surrender possible is the fact that you have boundaries and you also have the safety that is born from them. Then, the process of letting go of the boundaries and seeing the world beyond that becomes possible.

Similarly, we define ourselves in our sexual journey and claim ourselves. In the Mystic, we dissolve one more time. We are deconstructed to a different level to find ourselves again and yet different. Any encounter with the edges of ourselves and the edges of the universe transforms us.

The immensity of experiences that are available to the Mystic and the impossibility to contain them in our human form require the container to be as large as the universe itself. The only way that the body can contain the energy is by being a channel of all experience and for the personality to get out of the way. This sexual experience is physical, emotional, and spiritual—happening all at the same time.

At the door to the ceremonial space, you need to leave shame, any beliefs of being unwanted or being not beautiful enough behind. All those old monsters of our psyche must be cast away. In this moment of the mystical experience they are not present. What's left is our essence, not our sub-personalities.

The Shadow

The Shadow side of the Mystic is that you know how to be with God, but you may not know how to live in the day to day together easily. The Shadow of the Mystic is to have your head in the sky but to not have your feet on the ground.

There is a version of the Mystic which is disembodied, on a quest to transcend the body. In the sexual Mystic, the spiritual voyage is grounded in the physical body. That's why the opposite archetype, the Sensualist, is the anchor to the Mystic. It is the ground. Only by being deeply rooted in matter can we fly high and wide.

The pursuit of spiritual longing can be inebriating and consuming. It can be distracting from day-to-day purpose, including family, friends, partners, work, community, responsibility. The limitation for people is that they may forsake the world in a disembodied passionate way, another form of narcissism, a lack of presence rather than a vital awareness.

In the Mystic, people sometimes shun attachment to their partners under the pretext that the form "doesn't matter" and that true spiritual freedom is about nonattachment. This can be addiction. The constant search for sexual ecstasy can be another escape from reality and a strategy to avoid the difficult task of intimacy.

Promising spiritual enlightenment through sexual activity has certainly been the Shadow side of many spiritual teachers.

Another aspect of the Shadow is spiritual elitism that discards other experiences as not sacred. Some people hold themselves to be above others because of the training they have had. For example, "sexual magic" is not the only pathway to the spirit. It may be when you are most easily in touch with spirit, but that does not mean that all other work is not spiritual. Something as simple as holding hands can be profound. Our humanity is made of many pieces that fit together intricately. If you have all these "spiritual experiences" but you have no general tenderness or heartfulness in your daily life, then spirit is compartmentalized and is not alive through your whole life.

LESSONS

A journey into the Mystic offers the gifts of opening to the spiritual dimension within oneself and within the relationship. In the Mystic, you have moved from the personal to the collective or transpersonal. You have discovered the connection with all that is. You are transformed to serve not yourself, the family, or the tribe, but spirit itself. This is once again the paradox that can be difficult in relationship. If spirit is your Master, then where does your relationship, your family, and your tribe fit in? What muse do you follow? Is your relationship supporting your spiritual service? If so, it will survive and take many forms. Spirit doesn't care about which form a relationship takes, only that it is serving spirit.

The gift of the Mystic is to move beyond the physical appearance. As we get older and wrinkled, it is the archetype that allows us to look into each other's eyes at eighty years of age and see that this person is the most beautiful person in the whole world because in this moment we see beyond mere appearance. Any form is beautiful.

Another gift of the Mystic is the ability to surrender to the ecstatic dance—like a wave in the ocean where we become the wave and the ocean itself, where we become man and woman, and any creation.

Yet another gift is just to be at ease with the universe. To let the wind blow and embrace whatever situation comes our way. The Mystic learns that you cannot direct the energy, you can only dance with it. Only when we have the ability to surrender, will the door to magic open.

The Mystic connects us to the mystical dimension of life, to this reality that is always present at every moment even though we might not always be connected to it. Those mystical experiences reconnect us with knowledge that it is all right here. From one breath to the next, the gateway to the Divine is open to us.

The other thing that is healed is that in those moments of encounter with the mystical, our sense of separation disappears. For this moment we are whole, we are complete, and we are part of all. The more we experience that state, the more we can remember our sense of connectedness and belonging. That knowing can be with us in every moment.

The Mystic moves us beyond the pure attachment to the physical, to the form, to the place where we see beauty. In contact with the eyes that reflect the perfection of all things including ourselves, we become whole.

YOUR TURN

Here are some ideas to get started in the Mystic archetype:

- Find a tantra workshop, sign up, and go. Try www.tantra.com or www.Kreativeworld.com
- Make your space beautiful with candles and music
- Call in the deities, gods and goddesses, by name or description
- Make an invocation or a prayer to something that's important to you
- Imagine the most extraordinary sex possible and imagine tonight's the night
- Try eye gazing and breathing together
- Have sexual penetration with no movement, be perfectly still and quiet
- Come close to orgasm, then back off and be perfectly silent for a while
- Masturbate without coming
- Imagine moving your sexual energy from your genitals to your heart
- Make love really, really slowly for a long time
- Feel your inner body waves take over on their own

Onward

In the Mythic Journey, the mystical experience is the apotheosis; the place that we have been aiming at and longing for, the reward. This is where glory lives. Through the encounter with the Mystic and all other characters of the Pantheon, we are transformed.

Our heroes couldn't have gone through Heaven without experiencing all the other archetypes. They are in that way closely interdependent. The journey is not about the destination. It is about the moment-to-moment experience of what is presented to us and our response. The Mystic is also a teacher of nonattachment. And as any experience comes and goes, so we must open up ourselves to what is present.

It's a very paradoxical archetype. We can't live there because each experience has an end to it, and yet we can live there because we actually do experience it and the Mystic reality is always present.

CHAPTER NINE

Tending the Fire Anew

THE NURTURER

"Kindness, not wild abandon, is the essence of abiding passion."
— Anonymous

The Nurturer is about snuggling up on the couch, and enjoying that abiding closeness of a relationship well-earned and well-tended.

I realized that underneath even the most glorious sex, there is often a kind of pressure—more like a hunger—to press onwards. I love that I usually have the energy to do that. And so does Michelle. But slowing down with the Nurturer seemed like a kind of shortcut to sexual bliss. No heroics as with the other archetypes. We could just settle in and be together. That's all. No big fireworks, but no big mountains to climb over, either.

Oona warned us that the Nurturer might have its own surprises. But I was relaxed about it. Back to our couch.

— Michael

While Michael and Michelle are bicycling from Oona's couch to their couch at home, let's take a few moments for *you* to get comfortable in your favorite loveseat.

Do you love those long evenings of playing board games, or working on a jigsaw puzzle together? And later do you like to settle into bed, turn out the lights, and enter each other tenderly and slowly, without a whisper?

Do you like to just settle in with your mate, read books together side by side, occasionally getting up to refill your mugs with hot mulled apple cider? Do you sometimes like to get home in the evening, chuck your hardhat or briefcase right at the door and just collapse in bed together?

Or put on your pajamas before dinner just to feel the flannel kiss your skin. And feel your lover's warm hands slip silently under your nightie and stroke the small of your back, the tender nape of your neck right there on the living room sofa while you're gazing dreamily out the window at the setting sun.

Do you like just cuddling in bed? Holding each other tightly into dreamland, turning over together in your sleep during the night. Maybe making love in your sleep in the middle of the night. And remembering the best dreams in the morning.

If you do, then maybe this homey archetype is your home archetype. Or perhaps you are a restless explorer, but lovingly maintain a familiar "base camp" to return to from each wilderness expedition. Whatever your home archetype is, please do come home to the Nurturer now. Take loving care of each other. Stay home for a while. Enjoy the no-pressure, no-pain, lots-of-gain warmth of home and hearth. Feel your partner's arm wrapped around you snugly as you recline side by side, enjoying a calm, well-deserved respite from the cares of the world.

Here's a quick look at the low-keyed sexual electricity of the Nurturer:

- Snuggly, cozy, mutual, caring, easy, calm, sensitive, pleasing
- That exciting feeling of putting the key in the front door after a long trip
- Homey, comfortable, familiar, close, intimate, open
- Renewing, regenerating, re-sourcing
- A place where you can let down your hair, where a bad hair day is okay
- Where you feel like yourself, your regular self, where you can be yourself
- Grown-up version of being taken care of, can curl up and be "small"
- Giving, generous, mellow, sweet, gentle, tender, appreciative
- A refuge where you can touch, adore, love, and be loved

When you're "inside" the Nurturer archetype, you desire:

- Closeness, generosity, warmth, beauty, sensitivity, familiarity
- Reconnection, togetherness, tenderness, gentleness, comfort
- To be taken care of, to be given extra slack
- Fairy tales, bedtime stories ending in happily ever after
- Open-ended leisure time: no agenda, no goals, no pressure, no hurry
- To be touched, adored, and loved just because you're you

The most challenging task of the Nurturer is to invite Eros right into your home spaces—into the family room, into the kitchen. If you are in a long-term relationship, you probably know how easy it is to slip into a comfortable domestic routine. "Honey, did you bring in the groceries?" or "Sweetie, what would you like for dinner?" Daily life can be pleasant, but are you longing for that sizzle you had back when you were first dating? Remember the electric sparks shooting between you then?

Or maybe you *are* in a new relationship. Do you yearn for the ease and stability of simple evenings together at home? Are you contented just hanging out at home without needing to "do" anything? Are you worried that you might lose the fire in your relationship if life gets too habitual? That you might end up trading your juicy, fresh, newfound love life for a barren "platonic" friendship?

In either case, the Nurturer can be harder than it first appears. It can be very difficult to combine warm home life and hot sex, to create big enough space for both of the gods, Hestia and Eros.

SEX BACK AT THE "GRASS HUT"

Let's revisit the South Seas again to see some images of how you can brighten your home fires with more sexual heat, while always keeping your home base safe and protected. Maybe it's as simple as just moving into a grass hut. We'll see.

Last episode, in the Mystic, you ascended high above your tropical Island of Yes, arriving at its tallest mountain peak. You gazed out to the infinite horizon. All of the Island was visible from there, and perhaps the entire universe as well. Your spirit soared with the eagles. You drank the elixir of the gods. You spent the day entwined in intergalactic bliss.

Shadows are growing long now. You realized you are tired from doing so much lately: basking on the Island of Yes, adventuring out to sea and almost crashing your canoe on dangerous reefs, feasting with royalty, exploring dark caves, baking in the sun, all-night tribal dancing, and finally climbing this mountain peak yesterday. It is time to return home now.

You head back down the twisting path, through jungle and meadows, past verdant rain forests and prickly vines. Finally, you arrive back down on the beach. Your little grass hut, nestled in among the guava trees, awaits you with wide-open portal.

You enter the small open arch of the doorway into the small one room with its thick leafy mats, fuzzy blankets, and bright-colored pillows mounded up along the bamboo walls. You have only one single desire dripping off your sweaty, naked skin: to rest, relax, kick back, to inhale sweet breaths of still, sultry air while snuggling with your sweetie.

You take your partner's hand, kiss it tenderly, and reverently kneel before this treasured being. You look into each other's clear eyes. You motion your beloved to join you on the fragrant spongy bed of leaves and grasses. You wrap yourselves in blankets, surrounding your sprawled-out forms with pillows, tucking the supplest one under your heavy heads. Your bodies draw together on their own, all of them in one now familiar motion. The ocean waves match your breathing as you rock together in gentle sexual union. You relax into ecstasy. You are home now, sweetly, happily home together.

Sex in the Nurturer

Meanwhile, Michelle and Michael have just arrived home from Oona's office. They, too, have been through their versions of beach basking, dangerous reefs, royal feasts, dark caves, glaring sunlight, tribal dancing, and mountain climbing—seven sexual archetypes on their circuitous journey so far. Perhaps Michelle and Michael are looking just to kick back for a while.

♂ It had been a scorching day. When we got home, I wanted to take a nap, but I needed to check the houseplants to see if they needed watering. Michelle plopped down on the couch and flipped on the tube. A couple of minutes later on my way to the azalea, I glanced at Michelle, sprawled out like a limp French fried potato.

As I dipped my fingers in the moist soil under the tulips, I automatically shut out the drone of the TV.

Just then the TV chatter died. No sounds came from Michelle's direction. Did she accidentally roll over on the remote and nail the power button? Did Michelle's brain cells wilt on the parched desert of some Survivor rerun? I waited.

"Hey babe!" she called, "You didn't water the potted plant in the den…" Michelle was back. Maybe she got voted off the island.

I rounded the corner into the den, and realized I'd been voted onto the island. Michelle was wrapped in my favorite fuzzy blue blanket. Her bare arms were outstretched and so inviting. Somehow Michelle had remade our couch into our dream tropical island, the Island of Yes.

I slipped under the blanket to discover Michelle was naked. She stroked my face while she helped me get out of my clothes, too.

Michelle had our grass hut well stocked. She had a glass of water on the coffee table, a bottle of lube, and a bowl of guavas next to them. Michelle oiled me up and slid me inside her as easily as I'd dipped my fingers in that lush potting soil a few minutes before. Just like that. No foreplay. No nothing.

I can't explain it, but it felt totally, completely natural—as ordinary as pouring water on the tulips. And at the same time, the flood of pleasure almost made me pass out. I always think of sex as some-thing big, something I hunger for, something I get my expectations geared up for. But this was something else—the extraordinary inside the ordinary.

Michelle moved her hips in a slow, quiet rhythm. I felt so relaxed as her body enveloped me like we were tucked in a hammock, swaying to the breezes wafting off the Pacific. There was no tomorrow here, no alarm to get up for. I reached over and picked up a guava. I gently placed it in her open mouth. I gave her an extra love thrust as she chewed slowly on the succulent fruit. She gasped.

— Michael

In a way, the Nurturer is the "lost" sexual archetype. Movies portray sex as either exotic and romantic, or dangerous and violent. The media alternates between the untouchable beauty of sexy movie stars, and the sensationally sordid tales in the newspaper tabloids—with very little turf in between. It's little wonder that sex in ordinary homes can seem mundane by comparison.

Add to this seeming lack of glitz the work-a-day patterns we so easily fall into in home life, and you have a formula for domestic sexual emptiness.

But it doesn't have to be this way. As you can see with Michael and Michelle, the Nurturer is a very sexual, very sexy archetype. You just need to put on your Indiana Jones hat and become "Raiders of the Lost Nurturer."

Much of the zing of the Nurturer comes from the abiding surprise that sex can be normal and ordinary in a sense. Here sex is not just "normal" in the sense that it is healthy and good for you. Of course it is that. But in addition, in the Nurturer, sex is truly unremarkable, simple, and commonplace.

In the Nurturer, sex is downright *ordinary*. It's as ordinary as drinking a glass of water. Or as Michael says, sex is "as ordinary as pouring water on the tulips."

But here's the zinger.

At the same time, paradoxically, sex in the Nurturer is as extraordinary as any other sexual archetype. Sex is both *ordinary* and *extraordinary* at the very same time. In the Nurturer, sex is ordinary in the sense of normal, but never ordinary in the sense of average, run-of-the-mill, dull, humdrum, monotonous, or boring.

That's the key to the Nurturer: creating the *extraordinary inside the ordinary,* calling in the lyrical to animate the pedestrian, parking a spaceship in your two-car suburban garage, building a grass hut inside your modern urban den with a dartboard on the wall. The Nurturer demands that you keep your imaginations alive and inventive. You don't need an airplane ticket to spend a night in a grass hut. In a larger sense, the Nurturer is a continuing reminder that every tick of the clock, every breath we inhale is nothing short of a fantastic miracle.

So settle into that cozy loveseat, imagine you are far away in an exotic hideaway—just the two of you. And you are home. Safely at home. Here are a few tips to get you going. Sex in the Nurturer is:

- Natural, easy, comfortable, tender, relaxing
- Familiar, unpretentious, gentle, generous, mutual, caring
- Mellow, sweet, unhurried, familiar, calm, secure
- Snuggly, cozy, comfy, snug, sensitive, pleasing
- Loving, adoring, touching, fairy tale–like, happily-ever-after, warm and loving

Just because the Nurturer invites you to "make yourself at home," don't get out the vacuum cleaner or start talking about the life insurance policy that you forgot to renew. Like those leaks in the roof that Michael talked about at the beginning of this chapter, you can ignore crumbs on the floor and unpaid bills till later.

Enjoy becoming at home in the Nurturer. Here are a few things to remember as you rattle around your home.

- *Don't* answer the phone—you're home, but you're not home.
- *Don't* get busy with housecleaning and paperwork.
- *Don't* argue, judge, or be cynical.
- *Don't* break the tender mood.
- *Don't* refuse your partner's invitations or advances.

- *Do* be warm, comfortable, caring, affectionate, attentive.
- *Do* hug, say nice things, and give pretty flowers.
- *Do* be open to sex even if you don't think you want it, be willing, calmly eager.
- *Do* think out of the box, change your patterns, surprise each other, be provocative.
- *Do* slip off some extra piece of clothing if you have to vacuum.
- *Do* talk while having sex if you like, but paint word-pictures instead of ticking off facts.
- *Do* remember that you are alive right now, remind your partner of that miracle.
- *Do* look at each other, pay attention, touch, hold, and hug.

Your Arousal

In the Nurturer, arousal often comes seemingly out of nowhere. Michael was watering the plants when he came upon Michelle beckoning him to join her under the blankets. He didn't expect her to be nude. But he was open to the abrupt change of mood.

Sometimes arousal in the Nurturer can be shockingly direct and straightforward. "Honey, if you'd like me to give you head, I'd be happy to do that for you right now." Or the other way around, "Honey, I'm a little tired. Could you lick me for a few minutes to give me a quick energy boost?" In other archetypes, this kind of talk might seem forward, or even a bit rude. It certainly doesn't seem very romantic. But it's not crude. In the Nurturer, it's normal and easy, simple and direct. Sex is part of life, part of home and hearth, part of preening our bodies and staying healthy.

We can almost imagine a couple in the Nurturer saying over breakfast, "Sweetie, could you pass the milk for the cornflakes, wash your hands, and put your finger in my vagina." Okay, maybe that's a bit much, but you get the idea.

Erotic Fire

In the Nurturer, sexuality is alive but the burner is turned down low—dormant, but ready. It is a curfew time ("curfew" from the French for *couvre feu* or "cover the fire"). The erotic fire is banked, covered, protected, so as to last through the restful night to be rekindled once again in the morning. Indeed, this restful character is the sleeping night of our sexuality. Rather than being wildly sexual, it is sweet, easy, and direct.

A couple who lives primarily in the Nurturer archetype will say "we are best friends" but much of the time there is not a lot of sexual juice. You fall asleep spooning each other in a sweet embrace. You take off your pajamas to have sex. You aren't wearing your sexy lingerie.

In the sexuality of the Nurturer, you can really relax and be comfortable both in the body and in the soul. From this place of a sweet tenderness, sensation in the body can be felt deeply with an open heart. It's a good archetype to let go of shame because you feel loved, the body is accepted, open, and safe. You are in an equal power relationship. Humor is usually present in that space. The pacing of the lovemaking is spacious and has lots of room for being. It's liketaking a stroll in the country on a lazy Sunday afternoon. It's easy. There is a deep level of relaxation with who we are and with our partner.

Your Emotions

The Nurturer is the home of sweetness and tenderness. It's warm and connected. It's talking for long hours in a relaxed manner. When you are in the Nurturer archetype, emotions are heartfelt and expressed freely. There is no drama. There is something very precious about it. There is an emotional fulfillment that comes from giving, and nurturing those you love. The cup is full and being shared.

Your Orgasms

As you can imagine, the Nurturer is not exactly an archetype of orgasmic star-bursting fireworks. Nevertheless, a happy home is an inclusive home. So orgasms of all types and stripes are very welcome along with the rest of the fun things humans like to do at home.

And that's the key to orgasms in the Nurturer. They are natural, fun, light. There is no pressure to have an orgasm, just like there's no pressure to have chocolate sauce on your ice cream. Sure, chocolate sauce tastes good. But the ice cream is also quite tasty.

So, do welcome orgasms into the sexual repertoire of the Nurturer—however they happen. Orgasms are the symbol of the Everything that is good, the All that is beautiful. That's your home as it should be—a kind of sexual version of what Martha Stewart might advise on homes.

In the Nurturer, to welcome orgasms is to welcome the basic naturalness of sex. Even if you don't share sex with your guests, the spirit of the Nurturer is basic to having a truly hospitable home. It is the essence of hospitality. The wider the variety of people, feelings, opinions, emotions, etc., which are welcome in your home, the more your home will feel expansive, subjectively larger, grander. Homes are most fun to live in when they are well fortified like a castle, but within the protective outer walls there is much gaiety and full freedom of expression.

Now that you have a little better picture of the Nurturer, let's rejoin Michelle and Michael and see what is going on in their grass hut.

♀ It was sweet the way Michael stayed so deep inside me, lazily moving his lithe body in gentle rhythm to my rocking motion. My mind was so clear that I could think about exactly what was going on for me, every second. I might have even forgotten that I was having sex, except every so often a warm gush of molten lava would warm my core when Michael would move just slightly differently. But I never lost a thought-beat. I just rode through the pleasure waves and kept on noodling on this different kind of sex we were having.

Sex in the Nurturer was a lot like a long-term relationship. There was no particular beginning or end. It was more about just ambling along, like on a long walk on the beach, or a long-distance train trip. Usually, for me there's some pull toward an orgasmic finale. But not today. I felt like I could keep making love like this for hours.

And we had. I glanced over at the clock on the TV. We'd been in our grass hut for more than two hours, just gently swaying in our hammock, Michael hard and deep inside me. I was lying on top of

Michael, my feet poking out of the blanket, massaged by cool summer air. Occasionally, one of us would adjust positions just a smidge, and my whole vagina would catch fire, or my clit would get rubbed just so, and I'd see streaks of white-purple light blasting through my slowly mushing brain.

I thought about orgasms some more. I suppose some of those lava flows and white-purple light shows were a kind of low-keyed orgasm in their own sweet way. Who's to say they weren't? Still, they weren't what I was used to. And there was no sense of ending, like a musical cadence. It was more like Wagner's music where you never get a defining cadence, rather, the music just keeps going.

I hadn't expected the slowly building part. My mind was blurring up now. Strands of Wagner's music melted away. The bamboo walls of our grass hut were looking more effervescent, almost neon. What was happening?

Michael's familiar lips met mine and our tongues folded into each other. He was inside me, inside my essence. I opened more, and drew him deeper inside me. Please more, I screamed. Please enter me totally. This is where you belong. Inside of me. This is our home.

In a final surge of pleasure, I rolled over the top of one last joy wave, and collapsed on Michael's chest. Michael held me tight, wrapping his arms around my shoulders.

— Michelle

THE JOURNEY OF THE SEXUAL ARCHETYPES: COMFORTABLE SEXUALITY

You enter the Nurturer weary from our long arduous odyssey. You have worked hard and traveled through many archetypal landscapes and territories, each building or riding the erotic fire in new ways. You have thrived and survived through deep life-changing transformation. You have birthed yourselves anew. You have traveled a long way from the underworld to the stars. You have discovered the wealth of your inner erotic nature. You have earned your return to rest and renewal. The Nurturer is the place of stillness and simplicity, a place where one rests in the wholeness and completeness of oneself. It is a place where heroes and magicians can be human and simply let go and be. It is a place of peace, mindfulness of self and home. The Nurturer holds, soothes, and renews. They are the arms of the Mother Goddess, the Father God, benevolent and safe. In those arms, you are understood, comfortable, and seen.

The Nurturer and the one being nurtured are one. It's a dual relation but it is not polarized. It shifts back and forth between giving and receiving and it's happening at the same time. Part of being the mother or the father is that your wants and needs are being met as you are meeting another's wants and needs, selflessly and effortlessly.

It is a place of integration of the changes that have taken place. It is a place of gestation before the next cycle. Integration is a distillation of the experience and a deepening of experiences. It is a place of renewal before a new cycle, before a new adventure, before a new discovery. It is a place of preparation to spiral around a second, third, or seventh time to deepen the lessons of the archetypal landscape.

The Nurturer is into snuggling; everything's low-key, relaxing. The Nurturer's place is appropriately at the end of the voyage through the archetypes, because all of us desire rest after a long journey. In any good adventure tale, the hero returns home, empowered, tired, and exhilarated from the journey. So, too, the Nurturer signifies a return home. The Nurturer and the Magician share common ground, but where the Magician is deeply invested in helping the lover over a hurdle or through a lesson, the Nurturer is content to simply cuddle.

Our hero has traveled a long way—from the underworld to the stars. After the journey, it is time to return home, like Odysseus returning to the arms of Penelope in Ithaca. The Nurturer is the place of renewal, the place of emptiness and simplicity, where heroes and magicians can be human beings in simplicity.

The compassionate nature of the Nurturer is vital to developing a relationship with the Shadow aspects of all the archetypes. The Nurturer holds the place of the womb, the emptiness before the birth of new life, new awareness, new journeys, a new awakening of the life force. It's the home of long-term relationships.

How to Get Started

For the Nurturer, the daily life is itself a ceremony. It is the famous Zen saying of "Carry wood and chop water." The ceremony is present in the gestures of everyday life, in the smile across the room and a warm familiar embrace. It's time to lie on the couch, watch a good movie, and snuggle up by the fireplace.

You lie on the couch in close contact and talk about what's happening with the kids. There is something special about snuggling and talking about life while your legs are intertwined and you caress each other's faces as you speak.

Boundaries are not challenged and both partners make sure that the space of the relationship is safe. Basically, you are not going to come home from work and purposefully push the buttons of your partner. The safety is ensured by good communication, kindness, and consideration for each other.

As you prepare to meet the Nurturer, think about dressing down in your old pajamas and slippers or your favorite T-shirt thrown on top of your sweatpants. Wear clothes that make you feel comfortable and at home.

Costumes and Props

Nurturers may dress in pajamas or oversized, old T-shirts. They favor muted colors, low-key lighting, comfort foods such as puddings and stews, and relaxing music, or silence. Relax into the archetype of the Nurturer by snuggling up together in an old comforter, or piling a hammock with pillows and climbing in.

Setting the Stage

It is a Sunday spent in pajamas in front of the TV that gives us the ground to go in the world and move mountains. When you have that comfort, when you can roll around and be, you are better ready to face the world and its challenges. The Nurturer is like the womb, like the rich emptiness before the birth of new life, new awareness, new awakening.

In many other archetypes, the journey was about differentiating ourselves, finding who we are, breaking away from the society and tribe. In the Nurturer, it is a place where we belong, where we are known, where we are part of. It is the family, the home, the hearth.

For many relationships, the time spent in the Nurturer is the time that builds the safety in the container. The web of safety and trust that is established grounds a relationship and helps hold the tension of other archetypes. It is a vital part of a growing relationship. It is what makes you safe to push the edges, discover and open to experiences beyond your comfort zone. This is not glamorous. This is the beauty of the mundane.

The Nurturer doesn't flirt. The lover is welcome. Everything is clear and on the table. There is no sexual tension. The invitation is familiar…"Would you like a back rub?" "Let me take off your shoes and help get you comfy."

The Shadow

The Shadow of the Nurturer can be the inability to sustain the tension of differentiation. We are so alike, we think the same and feel the same that there is a lack of erotic tension, a loss of Eros. Nurturer-lovers can be like old couples who have let the fire go out and call each other Mom and Pop.

For some people, the Nurturer is a good strategy to prevent the encounter with conflicts that show up during high arousal when we encounter our sexual selves.

In the Nurturer, you can hide from expressing negative emotions directly to your mate such as anger, frustration, irritation, or rage.

The trap of this role is complacency and inertia. The Nurturer requires a paradox: while our sexuality is dormant, our deepest selves must remain wide awake.

LESSONS

A journey into the Nurturer gives us the gift of love. In the container where love flows, both the giving and the receiving fill us. There is a give and take between nurturing and letting yourself soak in the receiving of love. This archetype is the integration of love. The gift of providing the nurturing space for our partner is in fact a gift to ourselves to create safety in our life.

When a relationship goes through rocky times and difficult moments, the Nurturer will remind us of our commitment to the heart. Even in the times when we are not connected to love, we will remember that it always lives within us.

Your Turn

Here are some ideas to get you started in the Nurturer archetype:

- Try cuddling, cuddling, cuddling
- Get into your flannel pajamas
- Pile up your pillows into a love nest
- Give pleasure by pure generosity
- Cater to your partner, offer a back rub, or perhaps even to lick her or suck him
- Do something for your partner that you know that he or she really likes

Onward

The Nurturer brings us back to the simplicity of the present moment. The Nurturer in some ways is the end of a cycle, a time of completion, and the end of the mythic journey. We have heard the call. We have met the dragon. We have been transformed and we return home. There is a deep sense of inner peace. For a moment, there is nowhere to go, just being present to the wonder of carrying water and chopping wood.

It is from this contemplative place of quiet that we might hear the next call for adventure, and appreciate the fragility of our beautiful life and the special part of each moment.

CHAPTER TEN

Dancing with the Fire'

THE ARTIST

"To live as an artist is to share a part in the divine plan."
— Franco Zefirelli,
from *Tea with Mussolini*

Michael and I showed up at Oona's office early. Somehow all this sex we were learning about was overflowing into the rest of our lives. We were more together. I don't mean just closer as a couple. That was totally lovely. But also, we were more organized and focused. Our home is neater now. Michael doesn't leave his underwear on the floor anymore. Well, not as much anyway. And we get places on time, even early.

Now we were ready for the ninth and final sexual archetype. We told Oona to bring it on, whatever it was. Tell us what to do. Describe the cuisine. And we'd cook it up. Pronto.

— Michelle

Your Turn

Michelle and Michael have completed their work with Oona, and their tour of the archetypes—almost. They still have this last ninth sexual archetype to go. But the Artist is a bit different. Its central theme is freedom, artistic freedom. And integration of the other eight archetypes. We will see shortly what art Michelle and Michael paint with their bodies. In the meantime, what does your canvas look like?

Are you a free spirit? Do you listen to music with your body, moving to its beat, tapping your feet to its rhythm? Are you spontaneous in your sexuality? Can you switch sexual moods on a dime, change sexual horses mid-gallop? Is sex for you like finger-painting, where you don't know what it will look like until you're done?

If you walk through life in ballet slippers, if improvisation is your middle name, then perhaps the Artist is your "home" sexual archetype. If not, give yourself permission to be a free spirit for a few wild moments.

Here's a brief glance at the electricity which awaits you with the Artist:

- Natural, free spirited, wild-eyed, fluid, fluent sex
- Spontaneity, newness, freshness, wonder, beauty
- The energy of a wild horse, the power of a stallion
- Variety, versatility, carefree impulsiveness
- Unfettered, liberated creativity
- Touching, tenderness, connection, adoration, and love

When you're inside the Artist archetype, you just feel:

- Free

Yes, because you are free. All the time. The Artist archetype just confirms this truth.

♀ *I remembered our first session. I was hard on Michael for being an unimaginative, meat-and-potatoes guy when it came to sex. And I'd complained that he wasn't very present either back then. I guess he wasn't. But neither was I. I'm not sure which one of us was more out to lunch during that time.*

I had no inkling that sex could be fine cuisine instead of fast food, nor that there were so many ways of being sexual together.

We had been mulling over all eight sexual archetypes we'd learned so far in our minds, playing them like movies in our heads. Each one had its own unique twist and surprise. Each one nudged us in an unexpected way. They were like movies, except we were inside them. I'm not sure we'll get any academy awards, unless they create a new category for Best Orgasm.

Then I felt this funny leap in my belly. And a fluttery quick squeeze in my vagina. We must already know the answer. The next archetype has got to be staring us right in the face, jerking our chain. We've probably already stumbled into it. But what could it possibly be?

Michael said, "It's the movies! All of them. Those movies playing in our minds on the sexual archetypes. It's the whole enchilada! the artist is putting the archetypes all together, synthesizing them, integrating them."

The archetype of the Artist fell into place. This last archetype is about freedom—freedom we could never have imagined before, much less explored on our own.

The Artist is the celebration of the archetypes in continuous movement, the ecstatic dance of the human spirit, the jazz of the soul.

In the Artist archetype we are free to be whatever archetype calls our fancy. There is no plan. All of the archetypes are equally powerful and important to our sexual health and wholeness. In the Artist, we play the archetypes like musical instruments. Together they form the symphony of our sexuality.

We'd graduated with honors in sexual archetypes. We gave our-selves our own diplomas. And in a way, we had graduated early. We had all the knowledge we needed to teach ourselves about the Artist, and deepen our knowledge of the archetypes. We were our own professors now.

We said goodbye to Oona and were off to explore the ninth sexual archetype, the Artist. We knew what to do.

— Michelle

SEX AT SEA

The curtain is about to close on our South Seas adventures. As much as you have loved your sweet times on your beloved Island of Yes, your journey continues on. It's time to go. A large sailboat with its towering mast has entered your lagoon and has come to pick you up.

You and your sweetie wave your hands vigorously in front of your grass hut, still naked. In a flash, you both dive in to the warm, caressing waters. You swim strongly out together to this grand vessel and climb aboard, dripping wet. In minutes your yacht is heeling over into the wind, cutting through the waves. You hold hands and stare out into the blue-green Pacific waters.

You wonder where you are going, what will happen next. The Island of Yes with its daily intensity of dangers, feast, and dances is turning into a dot on the horizon. You promise to keep those experiences in your heart, and you do. You have been changed. You will never be the same again.

Just then your sweetie invites you to go below deck and make love right in that instant. You're still entranced by the bubbles of sea froth flying by on the waves, and the sea spray occasionally wetting your face. Your partner immediately senses your hesitation, understands perfectly, and returns to your side with a gentle salty kiss on your lips. The boat speeds along. Every so often, a fish jumps into the air. The sails billow and whip.

A slight chill enters the air as the sun nears the horizon. Now it is time to go below deck. You hold hands as you descend down the narrow ladder toward your small quarters. You yearn to make love, yet wonder just how to begin. It's as if all those eight ways you made love on the Island of Yes are jumbled, one on top of the other, and all calling your names in a cacophony. "Come, do it our way," each seems to entreat.

Then your skin touches skin, and fire enflames your loins. You remember. You know. You make love in a symphony of sensation, feelings, skin, and golden touch.

As we were arriving home, we both looked at each other and laughed. We still don't know what our 'home' sexual archetypes are! We forgot to ask Oona about that.

Does it matter? What matters is that we're at home in all of the archetypes now, at home alone together. We kissed and laughed again. We were home.

— Michael and Michelle

Afterglow

Congratulations on completing...
A Year of Sex Therapy in a Book

Welcome home from your odyssey of the nine Sexual Archetypes. We hope you enjoyed many mouth-watering feasts of fine sexual dining. Perhaps you even cooked up some of your own sumptuous creations as well.

In the pages that follow, we've included some space for your own notes and journaling. To get you started, here are some questions to ask yourself and your partner. You can use these questions for each archetype individually, or to help you sum up your whole "year of sex therapy."

- What was your experience like?
- Were you able to identify your own "home" archetype?
- If so, which archetype was it?
- Did you hit any bumps in the road, any hard places?
- Where did you feel confortable? Stretched? Confined?
- Where did you find your limits? What did you do
  with it?
- Did you feel like you had choices? Could you co-create?
- Were you changed, moved, renewed, transformed? How?
- What surprised you, captivated you, caught
  your attention?
- What did you learn about yourself? Did you get
  new insights?
- What's next on your sexual path? What is your
  heart's desire?
- Did you find new intimacy with your partner?
- Did you follow your bliss?

If there are particular nuggets you would like to share with us, we would love to hear from you. Please send them to us at JimAndOona@BlissInBed.com. We look forward to hearing your comments, thoughts, suggestions—and most of all, your stories of your adventures on your own "Hero's Journey" of these archetypes.

We think of these nine Sexual Archetypes as a kind of "alphabet" of our sexuality. In this book we have shown you each of the nine "letters" of this unusual alphabet, one at a time. To understand them more easily, we suggest that both partners practice the same "letter" or archetype at the same time.

But what if you mix them up? What if you and your partner engage each other from different archetypes? What if you combine different "letters" into new "words?" This is the "alchemy" of the Sexual Archetypes. This too can be quite delicious, intimate, and fun.

We are planning a follow-up book to explore this archetypal "alchemy"—what Michelle calls the "full freedom" of the archetypes:

♀ *Of course, that full freedom, just makes sex even hotter. Mostly, we can't keep our hands off each other. (Stop it Michael, I'm trying to type this letter!) He'll get what's coming to him in a second. I won't tell him what archetype I've got up my sleeveless dress.*

I wonder what Michael's cooking up for me, too. Or what's in store for both of us when these two surprise archetypes meet in a few tantalizing minutes. But we'll wait to tell you those yummy bedtime stories when we all meet again.

— Michelle

So, keep a diary of your experiences in the following pages. And tell us your bedtime stories.

May your sex be steamy and intimate, imaginative and creative, beautiful and heartfelt.

– Jim & Oona

THE INNOCENT

Her thoughts:

His thoughts

The Adventurer

Her thoughts:

His thoughts:

THE SENSUALIST

Her thoughts:

His thoughts:

The Seeker

Her thoughts:

His thoughts:

The Revealer

Her thoughts:

His thoughts:

The Magician

Her thoughts:

His thoughts:

The Mystic

Her thoughts:

His thoughts:

The Nurturer

Her thoughts:

His thoughts:

The Artist

Her thoughts:

His thoughts:

244

ACKNOWLEDGMENTS

We wish to express our gratitude to the many people who have supported and contributed to this book. To Sussanna Dimmitt, for pioneering the teaching of sexual archetypes in my women's group; to Alexandra Hart and Julie Mooney, for their editing and work on our book proposal; to Kate Thomas, for her support in developing this work. To Maren Pedersen, for her support and listening to early drafts being read out loud. Thanks to Paula Munier, our editor at Fair Winds Press, for her vision, patience, encouragement, and love of our work. To Wendy Simard, for her skillful and insightful copy editing. To Ken Atchity, our agent, for his navigation through the world of publishing. We'd especially like to thank the many people in our lives who have participated in our knowledge of soulful and enlivened sexuality: friends, lovers, and spouses. And finally, thanks to the "Q group," for its caldron of creativity.

About The Authors

JAMES HERRIOT, Ph.D., is a scientist, philosopher, teacher, and writer, with a special love for the mystery of the human creative process. How does it work? Theory. And how can each of us become more creative in our own lives? Practice. His theoretical work began at Stanford University as a computer scientist, and then expanded into complexity science, chaos theory, and cognitive science—"generative" sciences. In the theoretical realm, he gives many keynote talks, has testified before the US Senate, and heads up a company, Herriot Research (www.herriot.com). Exploring the practice of creativity, he focuses on human sexuality, researching human sexual behaviors, studying mythology, guiding doctoral students, teaching Tantra workshops—and writing books on sex.

Jim lives in northern California with his wife of 30 years, and their two children. He has lived in the USA and Europe, traveled to over a hundred countries, and converses in five languages.

ONA MOURIER, Ph.D., is an explorer of the many faces of the Self, a shaman, a wise woman, a visionary, a trickster and an entrepreneur. She has devoted her life to the exploration of the Mystery. Her innovative mind has lead her to create new paradigms in sexuality, as well as in relationships, business and new economic systems that can free people to fulfill their destinies, and enhance social and spiritual values. Oona's career is shared between her work as a sexologist and business owner in the health and fitness industry. Oona is a sexologist in private practice in Sebastopol. She is also the CEO of Sensual Signatures Inc. a business developing and producing sexual products (www.sensualsignatures.com). She has been lecturing nationally and teaching workshops on Sexual Archetypes since 1990. Oona is a Diplomate of the American Board of Sexology and Fellow of the American Academy of Clinical Sexology.

Oona is a practicing Buddhist and lives in Sebastopol, California, in an alternative family with her daughter. She has lived on four continents and easily crosses cultures bridging disparate traditions. She is fluent in four languages.

JIM AND OONA can be reached at:

www.BlissInBed.com
JimAndOona@BlissInBed.com

We welcome your stories, questions, and inquiries about upcoming talks and workshops.